DISCARD

WEST GA REG LIB SYS
Neva Lomason
Memorial Library

Redneck
Riviera

ALSO BY DENNIS COVINGTON

Lizard
Lasso the Moon
Salvation on Sand Mountain
Cleaving

Redneck Riviera

Armadillos, Outlaws,
and the
Demise of an American Dream

DENNIS COVINGTON

COUNTERPOINT
A MEMBER OF THE PERSEUS BOOKS GROUP
NEW YORK

for Jeanie

Copyright © 2004 by Dennis Covington

Published by Counterpoint,
A Member of the Perseus Books Group

All rights reserved. Printed in the United States of America. No part of this book may be reproduced in any manner whatsoever without written permission except in the case of brief quotations embodied in critical articles and reviews. For information, address Counterpoint, 387 Park Avenue South, New York, NY 10016

This is a work of nonfiction, but some names and biographical details have been changed to protect identities.

ISBN 1–58243–295–3

Counterpoint books are available at special discounts for bulk purchases in the United States by corporations, institutions, and other organizations. For more information, please contact the Special Market Department at the Perseus Books Group, 11 Cambridge Center, Cambridge, MA 02142, or call (617) 252–5298, (800) 255–1514 or e-mail j.mccrary@perseusbooks.com.

Library of Congress Cataloging-in-Publication Data

Covington, Dennis.
    Redneck Riviera : armadillos, outlaws and the demise of an American dream / Dennis Covington.
        p. cm.
    ISBN 1-58243-295-3
    1. Polk County (Fla.)—Social life and customs—20th century. 2.
Covington, Dennis. 3. Covington, Dennis—Childhood and youth. 4.
Covington family. 5. Polk County (Fla.)—Biography.
    6. Land tenure—Florida—Polk County—History—20th century. 7. Real estate development—Florida—Polk County—History—20th century. 8. Polk County (Fla.)—History—20th century.
    9. Birmingham (Ala.)—Biography.   I. Title.

    F317.P7C685 2003
    975.9'67—dc22

                                                                    2003014445

    Interior Design by Sagecraft
    Set in 11.5-point Sabon by the Perseus Books Group

03 04 05 / 10 9 8 7 6 5 4 3 2 1

Contents

I know that every good and excellent thing in the world stands moment by moment on the razor-edge of danger and must be fought for—whether it's a field, or a home, or a country.

—THORNTON WILDER

Prologue

The fat boys have killed a hog and are dragging it off the toolbox of their uncle's pickup truck, which is parked in the sun at a defunct Florida real estate development called River Ranch Acres. "We didn't mean to kill it," one of the boys explains. "We was gonna take it home and train our pups with it. But then the big dog, this one right here, ripped its ear off, and the others kept catching it by the throat. So we had to go ahead and kill it."

The dogs in the back of the truck start yapping, and the boy has to tell them to shut up. Four of the dogs are curs. The other two are red-nosed pit bulls. The hog itself is a medium-sized sow with long brown bristles that look as though they have been combed and parted down the exact middle of its back.

"You know the burnt-up bridge?" the boy continues. "We got stuck there and was washing off in a mudhole when the dogs took off into the palmetto bush and cornered the hog."

"We wasn't gonna kill it," the other boy insists.

The boys lift the hog by its legs and start half dragging, half carrying it toward a cement slab beneath a dangling set of scales at the side of the road. Both boys are shirtless and barefoot in the Florida sun. They lay the hog on the cement slab. Then they hoist it up so one of them can stick a metal hook through its hind legs. The scales creak with the weight, and blood begins to drain into an open pipe at the center of the slab. The animal has been shot behind the shoulder, and from the hole where its ear used to be, a piece of brain blossoms like a rose.

"He weighs eighty pounds," says one of the boys.

"There ain't no way this hog weighs eighty," the other one says. "These scales are lying. Wait till Franklin gets here."

Franklin Jackson is the boys' uncle. He's in the gatehouse of the nearby Hunt Club, where he has been registering the kill in a notebook that customarily hangs by the counter under advertisements for swamp buggies and camp stoves. The Hunt Club buys the hogs and pens and feeds them until the start of the season. Then it sets the hogs loose, to be hunted down by packs of dogs. The curs are trained to follow the scent; the pit bulls are trained to attack. The human hunter's role is less well-defined, except as armed observer of the melee and ultimate deliverer of the coup de grâce.

When Franklin Jackson steps out of the gatehouse, I can see he is a wiry, bare-chested man, with the initials "F. J." tattooed onto his right deltoid.

"Well, bust my bloomers!" he says as he squints at the numbers on the scale. Then he glances back at his nephews. "Pretty good work for a couple of fat boys."

And that's how he winds up recording the event in the Hunt Club notebook: *Sow. 80 lbs. 1-11-97.* In the space for the hunters' names, he has crossed out *Jackson* and written, instead, *the fat boys.*

The Florida Short Route

My father was color-blind. He couldn't tell the difference between certain shades of red and green. This caused him no trouble driving in Birmingham, where the traffic lights were red on top and green on bottom. But Dad had a problem when he drove us to Laguna Beach, Florida, for our family vacations. In the small south Alabama towns along what was then called the Florida Short Route, the traffic lights were reversed— green on top and red on bottom. So Dad ran red lights all the way to Florida.

My sister, Jeanie, and I didn't say anything. We just held on for dear life. We were afraid Dad might be sensitive about being color-blind, and we didn't want to embarrass him. Mother didn't seem to notice one way or the other. When we came within sight of the Gulf of Mexico, she was still worrying about whether she had turned the oven off back in Birmingham.

In Jeanie's first memory of these Florida vacations, three families drove down in an Army truck. I wasn't born yet, although I swear I remember the canvas sides of that truck flapping in the wind. The other families were the Hightowers and Weldons. There were six adults and twelve children in all.

The men took turns driving at night to avoid the heat, Jeanie says, and when one of them hit a wild hog outside Opp, Alabama, he pulled the truck onto the shoulder, and he and the others dragged the hog out of the road. I swear I was on that truck. Jeanie says, no, the first time I went to Florida, I was a baby and they tied my crib to the top of Dad's black Chevrolet. Jeanie remembers this trip distinctly, because the crib blew loose somewhere near DeFuniak Springs and went cartwheeling down the highway behind them.

My first memories of Florida are of a favorite beach toy—a blown-up Keystone Cop. There is a photo of Jeanie and me on the beach with it. Behind us are the legs of boys. The right side of the photograph, where I suspect my mother and father might have been, has been torn off. I cannot see the faces of my brothers, but I know them by their legs—Scotty's long and slender, like my father's; Gary's dark and muscular, like those of the actor James Dean. Scotty is sixteen in the photo, Gary is fourteen, Jeanie is ten, and I am two. Except for the Keystone Cop, I don't remember this trip, but I remember most of the ones that followed it.

There were always violent thunderstorms in Montgomery, and south of Montgomery, we saw the first windmills. In Luverne or Brantley was a Pure Oil station with a live oak tree out front. At the base of the trunk, someone had constructed an enormous cage and filled it with squirrels.

The streets of Florala, the last town before the state line, were lined with cabbage palms. Then we were in Florida. The land was flat, with truck farms and slash pine forests; the shoulders of the road were sand and broken seashells instead of gravel; and if we hadn't had car trouble by the time we reached DeFuniak Springs, it was a safe bet we'd make it all the way to the Gulf.

We used to stay in a rental cottage called the "Dottie Lou." It was a screened bungalow across the highway from the Gulf and just a short walk from the Seahorse, a combination grocery, cafe, and game room. Dad would often send Jeanie to the Seahorse for a Baby Ruth and Coke. I remember playing pinball there. It was on the stretch of beach in front of the Seahorse that Jeanie and I once watched a drowned man being pulled from the surf.

We didn't know the dead man, but the drowning made the Birmingham papers, an indication of the extent to which Laguna Beach and Birmingham were inextricably bound, although three hundred miles apart. Both the Dottie Lou and the Seahorse were owned by Birmingham families, and the closest other commercial establishment on the beach, a liquor store, was called the Little Birmingham. It had an enormous neon sign out front in the shape of our city's famous statue of Vulcan. In Roman mythology, Vulcan was the god of the fire and the forge, and so a fitting emblem of Birmingham's iron and steel industry. As husband of Diana, though, Vulcan was also Western civilization's most legendary cuckold, a fact the Birmingham Chamber of Commerce did not choose to advertise.

One of my dad's brothers, Uncle Charlie, owned the Bahama Beach Sundries farther down the beach. I remember the place as a narrow enterprise, with only one aisle. The walls were stacked high with canned goods and inflatable beach toys, and the counter racks held a wide variety of candies, including Fireballs, my favorite kind of jawbreaker.

Uncle Charlie had retired from his job as pressman at *The Birmingham News* and was confined to a wheelchair by rheumatoid arthritis, so his wife, Lillian, waited on customers at the store. She was a tiny Italian woman, devoutly Roman Catholic. I remember watching one day as she mounted the stepladder to retrieve a Sylvester punching bag from the top shelf. She had married into a contentious Covington family of twelve children who were nominally, if not rigorously, Protestant, and although I don't think Lillian ever encountered prejudice on this account, I do recall her and Charlie and their children being referred to as "the Catholic wing."

There were actually two Aunt Lillians in our family. Another of my father's brothers, Uncle Clarence, had married a woman named Lillian. We called them Charlie's Lillian and Clarence's Lillian. (Another of Dad's brothers, Uncle Victor, had a wife named Lillian, but we did not call her Victor's Lillian. We simply called her Aunt Bill.)

Between the Little Birmingham and Bahama Beach Sundries was a dance hall called Aultman's, where Jeanie says Bear Reeves and other Birmingham boys used to get into fights. Aultman's had a reputation as a dark, smoky place frequented by motorcycle gangs. The police tear-gassed it once. So Dad forbade Jeanie to go there at night, but one time he let my brother Gary take her there at four o'clock on a weekday afternoon. Already the jukebox was blaring, and the tables were occupied by tattooed bikers and their women. There was a lot of beer and dancing, but Jeanie says, "I think the fighting didn't start till after dark."

The popular record at Aultman's in those days was a cut by a Birmingham band. "I got the Panama City blu-ues," it began. "I been drinking too much bo-oze. Wah-oo . . . wah-oo." That same band later did a commercial for Skeets, the slacks that came in vibrant, solid col-ors—turquoise, scarlet, yellow, or green. "Skeets are neat, little Mama," they sang.

Aultman's eventually burned down.

But there were other places. Sometimes, Dad would let Jeanie go to the Hangout, a dance hall at the end of the pier at Long Beach Resort. She and her girlfriends would play arcade games while the music and laughter roiled around them like the surf. Jeanie was apt to have her hair in a ponytail and to be wearing one of Dad's white dress shirts with the shirttails out and her blue jeans rolled up at the cuffs. Between songs, if there was no breeze off the Gulf, she could hear the screams from the roller coaster ride at the amusement park across the highway. Jeanie doesn't remember dancing at the Hangout, only watching as older teenagers like Lefty Moore and Janet Alvis did the jitterbug and bop. The best dancer, Jeanie says, was a boy named Doug Porter. He has myasthenia gravis now. But in the late '50s, when Doug Porter stepped onto the dance floor, everybody else would stop and stand back to watch.

In the winter, the beach would be deserted except for shore birds and wild hogs, but after Memorial Day weekend, the cottages would be unshuttered and the water turned on. Floor mats would be shaken out. Bathing suits, towels, and dishrags would sprout on the makeshift clotheslines that someone had strung between mimosa trees. At night, lights would bloom in the windows of the cottages. Soon, they would be occupied by the families of vacationing steel workers and miners with names like Funston Parsons, Gilbert Hightower, Prude T. Cowan, and Fornie Hughes. And the wild hogs would shuffle across the highway and into the sandy side-streets—a good thing, my brother Gary says, because wild hogs were the only garbage collectors in Laguna Beach back then.

The beach was public, with no highrises or structures of any kind to block the view from the roof of the Seahorse, where Dad and I would sometimes climb to share a Dr. Pepper. Down on the beach, children trudged into the surf dragging their black inner tubes behind them. Mothers in one-piece bathing suits spread blankets, unpacked picnic baskets, and craned their necks to spot their children's heads against the pale green of distant sandbars. While the women worked, the fathers trolled for sea bass, but they typically caught only rooster fish, a deranged-looking species whose members croaked audibly when pliers were applied to their tail fins.

Except for the spectacle of teenagers clowning around in the surf, which Dad thought dangerous and unbecoming, Dad found this setting perfectly suited to the play of his imagination. "Back in the thirties," he said, "I could have bought this beach for a dollar a foot." He neglected to mention that in the thirties, neither he nor anyone he knew had a dollar to spare on a pair of extra shoes, much less a patch of sand three hundred miles from Birmingham. But I knew Dad wasn't really thinking about money as he sipped his Dr. Pepper. His eyes were fixed on the horizon, where the vastness of sea and sky met in a seamless perfection that he said confirmed his belief in God.

Dad's parents had never even seen the ocean. Their people had come down from the mountains after the Civil War to find work in the foundries and railroad yards of Birmingham. Dad's generation was the first one urban-born, and he was proud to have risen to a supervisory position in production planning at Tennessee

Coal and Iron, later bought by U.S. Steel. So he considered a Florida vacation something special, a sign of his generation's upward mobility. But there proved to be nothing really upward about it. We always stayed at the same kind of place, either the Dottie Lou or the Shangri-La or the Bide-a-Wee, cottages with unvarnished plank walls and sofa beds. I slept on an interior window stool that had been extended into a kind of bunk, a nesting spot insufferably hot during the day but cooled at night by breezes from the Gulf.

The water in these cottages tasted like sulfur, and there were enormous flying insects, mildly poisonous toads, and frequent plumbing or electrical crises, all of which Dad handled with unruffled patience, as though he suspected we didn't deserve better, considering where we were from. "Defugalties," he called these irritations before he picked up the pipe wrench or opened the fuse box. During lengthy power outages, we lit candles and played Parcheesi or Rook. And instead of moving up to better quarters, my family, after Jeanie got married, stopped coming to the beach altogether.

But in the '50s, when we still went to the beach, there was always somebody there we knew. It might be Pat and Molly Stevens and their girls. Pat Stevens was Dad's closest friend, a red-haired talker who pulled quarters from my ears. Pat's stories might be about the bureaucratic idiocies of the post office where he worked, or the genius of Scooter, his dog, or an indignity he'd recently endured—the doughnut-shaped cushion he had to sit on after hemorrhoid surgery, for instance. But most of Pat's stories would turn ultimately on what he saw as my father's peculiarities: Dad's moral rectitude, which Pat saw as squeamishness; his reluctance to haggle over the price of cars, which Pat thought foolish and un-American; and his total disinterest in professional sports, about which Pat would simply throw up his hands in dismay.

Dad was such a stickler for details, Pat said, that he would continue to follow directions after he knew for a fact they were wrong. "Do you know how many days it took Sam to assemble your bicycle?" he'd ask me. No matter what I answered, he'd say, "Guess again." And Pat was unmerciful about the words Dad routinely mispronounced: "sympathy orchestra" for "symphony orchestra," or "jynecologist" for the doctor who specialized in "women's problems."

Once Pat gave my father an aqua ashtray that he'd bought in a Panama City, Florida, souvenir store. Dad never used the gift for cigarettes, but kept it handy on an end table in Birmingham because he said it smelled like Florida to him. He would hold it out to me. I'd take a deep breath and agree with him. It smelled of suntan lotion, eucalyptus leaves, and the aftermath of thunderstorms.

Another couple we'd see in Florida were Sara and Fornie Hughes. Sara was Mom's best friend. I loved the way she laughed. Her husband, Fornie, drove a Buick and smoked cigars. A souvenir that Fornie bought in

Panama City was a miniature alligator made of metal and painted green. When Fornie pushed the alligator's tail, its mouth would open, and the head and shoulders of a recently devoured black boy would appear. Fornie found this toy enormously entertaining, but Dad seemed not to see the humor in it. "Not that there's anything wrong with Buicks," he'd say after Sara and Fornie had left.

And then there were the Hydes. The mother, Mattie Lou, worked for Dr. Day, our local optometrist, and her husband, Ramsey, had a flattop haircut just like Gus Grissom's. The Hydes' son, Roy, went to Woodlawn High School with Jeanie. My whole family, including me, wound up going to Woodlawn. Roy sang in the Warblers, the boys' glee club, which Jeanie accompanied on piano under the indignities of the club's director, a little body builder named Joe Turner, who also was a lifeguard during the summers at Cascade Plunge.

Every year the Warblers put on a blackface minstrel show that was the highlight of the school year. They sang songs like "Blue Indigo," "Sentimental Journey," and "Oh, Mona." They wore bow ties and coats with tails, and they would sit in a circle on stage in chairs from under which they would take straw boaters, canes, and cut-out banjos for their biggest numbers, which they performed under black light so that the shirts their mothers had washed in Tide could glow in the darkened auditorium. The group had an "interlocutor," the only member not in blackface, who would be the straight man for all the jokes, and the end men, the comedians, would be dressed like field hands or bums. The jokes were low humor, often with a slightly racial twist. "So you say your car broke down?" Mr. Interlocutor might ask. And an end man would reply, "Yassuh, the carburetor wouldn't carb, and the generator wouldn't gen, and the pistons wouldn't . . . well, *dey* wouldn't work either!"

To be a Warbler was to be at the top of the high school pecking order, more notable even than being a member of the football team or student council. Such was the demand for admittance to the group that prospective members had to endure an initiation in which they faced The Machine, a device that applied electric current to the initiates' testicles. Why members of a high school boys' glee club should apply electricity to one another's testicles remains a mystery to me. But I do know that Joe Turner took his Warblers to Panama City every summer, where Jeanie says he would strut around in his bikini bathing suit and show his strength by lifting everybody onto his shoulders.

Purists will insist that the term "Redneck Riviera," which was coined by former University of Alabama and Oakland Raider quarterback Kenny Stabler, refers only to that stretch of Alabama Gulf Coast between Fort Morgan and the Flora-Bama, a lounge that straddles the state line. (The big event at the Flora-Bama is an annual mullet toss.) But those of us who vacationed on the Florida side of the border recognize that restricting the term "Redneck Riviera" to the Alabama side is at best a case of splitting hairs, and at worst a display of interstate rivalry and regional prejudice.

I mean, we were all from Alabama anyway.

In June of 1959, my mother actually did leave the oven on in Birmingham. We were halfway to Florida, at a town called Highland Home, when she remembered she'd left a ham baking on the bottom rack. So Dad turned the car around, and we drove all the way back to Birmingham to retrieve it.

This was the summer after Dad had bought his first brand-new car, a 1959 Chevy Impala with that mean, swept-back look. The roof extended slightly beyond the rear window, and the fins curled down like wings. The killer, though, was the color: fire-engine red. My mother had begged him not to take Jeanie car hunting with him. She was eighteen and not to be trusted. But Dad took her anyway, and they came home with that sporty Chevy Impala. Mother was furious, but Dad just shrugged. How could he have known? He was color-blind.

Again, Scotty wouldn't be coming to Florida. He had his own family, a son who was a toddler now, and a job at Hayes Aircraft. Scotty had gotten married when I was five, so I knew him primarily by the artifacts left in his room: model airplanes of World War II and Korean vintage, strung from the ceiling so close the wings nearly touched; orange and blue Auburn pennants; jacks and marbles; Boy Scout badges; and a bookcase he had made by hand, carefully sanded and shellacked and with his initials tattooed in metal on the ends.

My other brother, Gary, was in the Army and stationed at Fort Sam Houston in San Antonio, Texas, so he wouldn't be coming to Florida, either. Like Scotty, Gary was more legendary than real to me—the boy who had almost died of scarlet fever and who had once received what Mom called "a lick on the head." Gary doesn't remember hitting his head when he was a boy. Of course he may have forgotten. I remember hitting my head, when I stepped in the way of Mother's broom while she was sweeping the kitchen, but I remember it only because she gave me two teaspoons of paregoric afterward. From then on, I tried to get in the way of Mother's broom as often as possible.

At least I had memories of Gary living with us. And when he'd come home on leave from the Army, I'd sit in his lap and box his upheld palms while he grinned and said, "Aw come on, you can do better than that."

It was no surprise that my brothers wouldn't be with us in Florida. But it was a surprise that this time, instead of one of Jeanie's girlfriends, like Susan Lawler or Sara Francis Hughes, we were taking our cousin Johnny Busby with us.

Johnny was a couple of years younger than Jeanie but still considerably older than me, so I had mixed feelings. Jeanie was engaged to marry Bunky Wolaver in September, right after she turned nineteen, and I didn't think it proper for her to spend so much time with

Johnny Busby, even if he was our cousin. Besides, she should have been spending the time with me. It was bad enough that she was going to leave me in September.

My parents' logic was that because Johnny's father had "taken a powder," or deserted him and his mother when he was a child, he had never had the opportunity to visit Florida the way we had. That was all fine and dandy, but as a practical matter it meant that Jeanie and Johnny would be tooling along the beach road toward the lights of Panama City with the windows of the red Impala rolled down and Pat Boone's "Love Letters in the Sand" playing on the radio, while I ate ham sandwiches with Mom and Dad on the picnic table of the un-airconditioned kitchen of whatever cottage Dad had managed to rent. This year, it was one of what were called Howell's Cottages.

On the way to our cottage, I wanted to stop and try my swing at the batting cages.

"You can do that at home," my mother said.

"What about carpet golf?"

"We have a Putt-Putt back in Birmingham," she said.

"Skee-ball then?"

"Some people bet on games like that."

"I wouldn't."

"Think of something educational," she said.

This was a stumper. You didn't come to Florida to get an education.

"Oh, I'll just go to the beach and swim," I said.

The words were out of my mother's mouth before she even knew it: "You can swim at home, at East Lake Park."

Of course, the first thing Dad did every summer was slip into his bathing trunks and start running down the dunes toward the beach. Mom stood at the highway and yelled for him to stop: He would underestimate the undertow; he would have a heart attack. Dad kept sprinting toward the surf, dived headlong into the first big wave, and came up shaking the glistening drops from his hair.

"Come on in," he'd shout. "The water's warm." Only later would we see the goose bumps on his arms and chest.

Mother couldn't stand the cold, but despite her talk about being satisfied with the water at East Lake Park, she would swim in the ocean early in the morning, before the rest of us were up. She said the water was as smooth as glass at dawn, and she loved to do the side stroke in calm water. Sometimes Dad and I would get to the beach in time to see her wading out of the Gulf, tugging off her rubber bathing cap and letting her blond hair blow loose in the wind.

At moments like these, I understood why, in this lovely but transitory world, there had wound up being a Scotty, a Gary, a Jeanie, a me. My mother and father were different—as different, in ways, as separate species—but they both loved to swim in the ocean, in

June, when it finally didn't matter whether the oven had been turned off back in Birmingham.

The last of my childhood vacations to Florida was the educational one my mother had always talked about, not to Laguna Beach but across the state to St. Augustine on the Atlantic Coast. I remember standing by a cannon in a fort made of crushed seashells. "This is history," Mom said. But the rest of the trip is a blur except for our visit to the Ross Allen Reptile Institute at Silver Springs, near Ocala, Florida, the dead center of the state.

It was here that Ross Allen himself asked for a volunteer from the audience to assist him with a five-foot-long indigo snake. I answered the call, and Mr. Allen draped the snake around my neck. The animal was heavy and serene, lovely in the descending light, and I was as ecstatic as boys are apt to get in public. The moment seemed to stretch forever—me, the snake, my adoring parents, and an amphitheater of anonymous admirers— and when Ross Allen finally lifted the snake from me, and I retook my seat, I was convinced that I had just experienced the high point of my life. This was my idea of an education. But afterward, I went to see the alligators, and I learned that education had another side.

It was feeding time. I was the only witness. Mom and Dad had gone to find a pay phone to call Gary and let him know when we'd get back to Birmingham, so they didn't see the man in thick boots and waist-high rubber waders as he entered the fenced enclosure and began emptying buckets of dead fish into the moat around the alligators' island. Until that moment, the alligators had looked exactly like those at the Birmingham Zoo. They had been as motionless as stone gargoyles. Dragonflies seemed attached to their snouts. But when the first dead fish hit the water with a slap, the alligators came to life. They crawled and bellied into the moat, where they began an underwater ballet that quickly accelerated into a frenzied race until a lucky few found the fish and brought them to the surface in a shattering of water and light. Then the rest of the reptilian mob erupted in a bedlam of appetites—snapping mouths, lashing tails, an orgy of brutishness that was the antithesis of the placid indigo snake draped across my shoulders. I even preferred the caged and frantic squirrels at the Pure Oil station in Brantley, Alabama. In their scramblings, the squirrels had at least seemed reasonable. They were trying to think things through and find a way out of the mess they'd gotten themselves into. They were like me. The alligators were like nothing I'd ever seen before—or ever wanted to see again.

The years after that final visit to Florida were not good ones for my father. After thirty years with U.S. Steel, he had been forced into early retirement to make way for a college graduate. The grief and depression over losing his job took on an aura of temporary insanity. First, Dad bought a VW Beetle on credit. (He'd never bought anything on credit before, and as a U.S. Steel employee, he'd sworn never to drive a foreign car off the lot.) Then he surprised us even more by purchasing the corner grocery store a block and a half from our house.

Covington Groceries.

Dad hadn't worked in a grocery store since 1929, the year he graduated from high school.

There were problems from the start at Covington Groceries. Dad extended credit to families that he knew would never be able to pay him back. He refused to sell beer and wine, losing business in the process to Pete Annella's father's store three blocks away and to the convenience chains sprouting up on First Avenue North. Finally, and perhaps most important: Dad's bananas were always overripe.

In taking to grocering so late in life, Dad seemed to be refighting, on a minuscule scale, the old battle between the Anglo-Irish and the Italians for control of Birmingham's fresh produce market, a battle the Italians had long since won. So by the end of that year, the store Dad had bought with such high hopes failed. He sold it to a furniture reupholsterer. And with the proceeds from that sale, just when we thought he might be returning to his senses, Dad made a down payment on two and a half acres of land in central Florida that he'd never seen.

I can't explain this bizarre behavior, except to say that it was 1965 and Dad was fifty-three, that age at which American men are assumed to be at the height of personal power and professional success. Instead, Dad had lost his job at U.S. Steel, had failed nobly as a friendly grocer, and was now delivering prescriptions part-time for a drugstore in the neighborhood where he had grown up.

That fall, he received an invitation to a dinner at our local Holiday Inn. The dinner was hosted by Gulf American Corporation, soon to become the largest land development company in the United States. Gulf American wanted to share, with a few select men of outstanding character, exciting news about a 44,800-acre development in Florida called River Ranch Acres.

River Ranch, as the company representatives explained during a slide presentation, was located halfway between Tampa on the Gulf Coast and Vero Beach on the Atlantic. It represented a Florida little known to the tourists who crowded both coasts, even though it lay along the main east-west highway across the state, Highway 60, and was only nineteen miles from the retirement city of Lake Wales and fifty miles or so from the coming attractions of Disney World in Orlando. Right in the path of progress, the representatives said.

Affordable, too.

For the most part uninhabited, except for cattle ranches and the Avon Park Air Force Range to the south, this vast swath of Florida, part of what was called the Osceola Plain, looked in the slides more like the flatlands of the Dakotas than it did the terrain of a conspicuously southern state. Roughly half of the land was prairie, where cattle grazed and bald eagles soared overhead and the sunsets were unspeakably beautiful, like those of the American West.

But once the westbound traveler came within sight of the Kissimmee River's tree line, he would realize he was entering a new place altogether. Rising out of the Osceola Plain, between the Kissimmee River on the east and Arbuckle Creek on the west, was a ridge twenty-one miles long and three to four miles wide. "Bombing Range Ridge" it was unpoetically called, simply because parts of it had once been used for target practice by the fighter bombers out of the Avon Park Air Force facility (a fact the company representatives mentioned but did not dwell on). The ridge's highest point was only 145 feet above sea level, but by Florida standards, this was a significant elevation.

"Bombing Range Ridge"—the heart of River Ranch.

Geologically, the ridge represented an anomaly, a marine sandbar created eons ago by the Atlantic Ocean, when this part of Florida had been a narrow spit of land separating a lagoon on the west from the ocean on the east. Ironically, the ridge, prairie, and wetlands that Gulf American bought and marketed as River Ranch Acres may have at one time been choice oceanfront, a prehistoric Daytona or Pompano Beach, since left high and mostly dry as the ocean receded and yielded up the land. But even without an ocean nearby, the landscape seemed to have promise, a wild, open beauty that could not have been entirely lost on the Birmingham diners that night.

There were other men Dad knew at the dinner, including his old friend Paul Hemphill Sr., a Birmingham boy of modest means like himself. I don't know exactly what happened after the dinner and slide presentation, other than that both Dad and Mr. Hemphill must have expressed more than usual interest in River Ranch Acres, but I can imagine Dad driving home that night in his blue VW. He would have been drawing deeply on one of his Lucky Strikes, or perhaps he had already switched to Half & Halfs, an even more potent brand that was half cigarette tobacco and half pipe tobacco. He always dropped his used matches onto the floorboard of the car.

On this drive, I imagine that Dad was in a hopeful, satisfied mood. I have known such times myself, when the world, despite the beating it has given you, relents for just a moment while you dream your exotic, defiant dream. Life won't take all of you, by God. You will salvage something from this mess and call it your own. You will put your name on it. You will have it signed, sealed, and delivered to the courthouse in the appropriate county of the appropriate state. It will be your private garden, the place where your imagination can play. In my father's case, it was two and a half acres of this land he'd never seen except in photos but was now tempted to buy from a salesman named Ray Chase after dinner at a Holiday Inn. Dad had never met Mr. Chase before, but the salesman seemed to understand exactly what Dad wanted: an investment, they would call it.

Inwardly both men must have winked at the word. I never heard Dad say an unkind thing about Mr. Chase, whom he probably saw as a hardworking, church-going man like himself, just trying to make ends meet, feed a family, keep a sense of dignity in troubled times.

It would be inappropriate for me to speculate about what Mr. Chase thought of my dad. Surely, he'd met many such men on his journeys back and forth across America—decent men, and some, easygoing and likable like my father: a prudent listener, a thoughtful, unskeptical sort. But mostly the diners at the Holiday Inns each night constituted a homogeneous lot, a generation of men who had come of age during the Great Depression, made their leap to the middle class, survived the second great war of the century, raised their children, moved into their final house, and now, in their early fifties, dreamed of possibilities beyond the practical demands of keeping a family afloat. Like Dad, they had played by the rules—stuck with the company, paid their taxes, bought life insurance, burial policies, savings bonds, their first new cars—and they now stood poised at that most powerful and vulnerable time of life, when the major financial obligations have been met but the great journey toward death has not yet fully begun, and the cracks that are beginning to show beneath the feet—the rumors of ill health, the decline in sexual vigor, the crises of adult children—serve only to propel the dreamer faster and further toward the cry of the one on the far ridge who has seen that elusive and ineluctable something that has until now been missing in life.

River Ranch Acres.

I could tell by the way Dad hooked his thumbs into his belt loops when he said the words that he liked the sound of the name. He'd never been west, but he loved western movies, and the brochures Mr. Chase had handed out at the dinner depicted couples on horseback, or laughing around campfires and circled chuck wagons.

"Saddle up!" the brochure proclaimed, and it was clear from the photos that the showplace lodge the company had built at River Ranch had a rustic, western feel—exposed beams, stuffed game on the walls, and spurs, revolvers, branding irons, bridles, and sheriffs' badges embedded like bees in amber in the laminated registration desk.

In retrospect, I think his buying the property at River Ranch was just a logical extension of all those red lights he'd run on the way to Florida. Dad was never happier than he had been on our family vacations to Laguna Beach. Maybe he thought he could buy back that happiness for good.

A Better Tomorrow

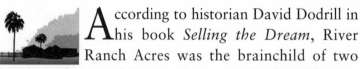 According to historian David Dodrill in his book *Selling the Dream*, River Ranch Acres was the brainchild of two brothers from Baltimore, Jack and Leonard Rosen. Dodrill says the Rosens were former carnival pitchmen who had made a small fortune selling Formula No. 9 hair creme on national television. They implied in the commercials that the lanolin contained in Formula No. 9 could grow human hair. They also pitched home appliances, children's vitamins, and diet pills that "expanded in the stomach, causing the user to eat less."

During these early days, the Rosen brothers honed two techniques that would later prove successful in their land business. The first was the hard sell, the ruthless barker's cry, that seductive combination of praise and shame that would lead otherwise level-headed, practical urbanites to plunk down good money for unimproved land they'd never seen a thousand miles away.

The second was the use of installment buying, which the Rosens introduced in their home appliance enterprise. With a small down payment, the buyer could take home a brand-new refrigerator and a string of monthly payments that stretched like a hall of mirrors into the future. The ultimate total cost of the refrigerator was not as apparent or troubling as the advantage of low payments over time. And if consumer items like appliances could be bought on time by the middle and lower classes, why not raw land, traditionally the private reserve of the gentry?

The Rosens' cosmetics company, Charles Antell, had made them millionaires, but competition in cosmetics was growing stiff. And Leonard Rosen had developed health problems that dictated a move to warmer climes. A lot of people, he learned, were making barrels of money on land sales in the Sunshine State. So he and Jack decided to sell the cosmetics company and begin looking for land in southwest Florida, a still largely undeveloped area where prices were cheap.

In 1957 the Rosens incorporated their land company, Gulf American, and purchased more than 1,700 acres west of Fort Myers. They paid roughly $400 an acre and subdivided the land into thousands of parcels that they sold mostly to fellow Easterners for between $900 and $3,400 each. The Rosens promised potential buyers a city there, a place they would call Cape Coral. Within a year, sales had passed the $9 million mark.

Buoyed by this early success, the Rosens plowed money back into the project, for additional land, roads, utilities, dredging operations, and the building of recreational facilities. The end product was the city the Rosens had promised. But Leonard and Jack couldn't resist the lure of an innovative—and more profitable—pitch. With Cape Coral, they had bought and sold practically worthless Florida land at an enormous profit, and in the process they had built a city. Now, instead of repeating themselves, why not up the ante? Why be satisfied with a margin of profit lessened by the cost of improvements to the land?

This was the reasoning, Dodrill says, that led to the Rosens' next development, Golden Gate Estates. It consisted of 112,000 acres northeast of Naples in Collier County, all bought for less than $200 an acre. This time, though, the brothers didn't prepare the land for home building, as they had at Cape Coral. Instead, they plowed unpaved access roads into the property, blasted twenty-four miles of canals, and started selling the raw land in five-acre parcels. In little over a year, they had sold 20,000 of these parcels. At Cape Coral, they had promised a city. At Golden Gate, they had hustled raw land with access roads in the hope of an eventual city. Both ventures were hugely successful, although the investment risk was falling increasingly upon the shoulders of the potential buyer.

By the third major project, River Ranch Acres, the Rosen brothers had abandoned altogether a sense of responsibility to the potential buyer. Dodrill says they described their idea as "revolutionary." Why not forget the land and how it might be used? Why not forget the customer? Why not go for the ultimate pitch? Why not just sell the dream?

The entire 44,800 acres at River Ranch was subdivided in a grid pattern, as it had been at Cape Coral and Golden Estates, so as to ensure the most lots per acre, in this case eight lots on every two and a half acres. That made a possible total of more than 140,000 lots, each within the quarter-acre range that permitted septic tanks should the lots ever be developed, a possibility Gulf American never envisioned for itself.

Although the company had divided the land on paper into these lots of 70 feet by 140 feet, it admitted in a Florida Public Offering Statement that the land was not being offered as a homesite subdivision at all. Instead of being individually surveyed, the lots would be sold within one-and-a-quarter-acre parcels that could be described legally by section, township, and range. In this way, land that Gulf American had bought for around $150 an acre could be sold for more than $1,000 an acre with no development costs other than the construction of the showplace lodge, golf course, RV park, marina, rodeo ring, western-style gift shop, and saloon, all of which had the outward impermanence of a movie set.

River Ranch was, in real estate parlance, a "paper subdivision." In this sense, it wasn't real at all. The only place it existed was on paper. In order to seal this deception, officials from Gulf American arranged a meeting with Polk County commissioners at John's Restaurant in

Bartow. When a Gulf American vice-president and the company's chief engineer, Thomas Weber, explained how the land was to be subdivided and marketed, the county representatives strongly objected. There was no way Polk County could afford to maintain all those new roads in the subdivision. Not to worry, the Gulf American officials insisted. They had no intention of ever building any roads. The subdivision would stay where it was—on paper. So the county, eager for the millions of property-tax dollars it would receive from the absentee parcel owners, accepted Gulf American's assurances there would never be roads to maintain. The commissioners essentially looked the other way while Gulf American subdivided the land into parcels that contained over a hundred thousand homesites and then sold them to the public while assuring the county there would never be any roads servicing those sites.

The parcels at River Ranch not only had no roads but also had no electricity, no drinking water, and no sewage system. Twenty percent of the parcels were under water. But that did not seem to discourage potential buyers, few of whom ever saw the actual piece of property they were buying and some of whom were never sent, or overlooked, the fine print in the public offering statement.

It wasn't until the Rosen brothers tried to sell land that was completely under water, at a so-called development called Remuda Ranch Grants, that the national press prodded state and federal regulators to take a closer look at the company's practices. The Rosens quickly sold Gulf American to GAC, a Pennsylvania-based finance company that declared bankruptcy in 1975. By then, Jack Rosen had died of a heart attack, but he reportedly had left an estate worth more than $10 million. Leonard Rosen lived to be seventy-two, and although he continued to be involved in shady land schemes in Nevada and elsewhere until he was convicted of income tax evasion, he, too, left an estate in excess of $10 million.

The roughly 16,000 property owners at River Ranch Acres, meanwhile, were left with nothing but the raw, unsurveyed, and unimproved land they had purchased at exorbitant prices nearly twenty years before. And as Dad began discovering to his dismay, even the land was in the process of being stolen from them.

It is 1982. Dad slides a copy of the latest River Ranch Landowners Association newsletter across the kitchen table to me.

"Look at this," he says.

The association has been founded by a retired union president named Dick Powell to protect the interests of legitimate River Ranch landowners like Dad and inform them about what is happening to their property. The news is seldom good, a fact that seems to make Dad's thyroid condition even worse than it was before. He has lost weight, his eyes are bulging, and his chin is set as though it has been chiseled that way. He has long since been diagnosed with emphysema, but he isn't on oxygen yet. He just always gets a little breathless when he talks about his investment down at River Ranch.

"You just read what they're doing down there," he says.

And to my mother, he adds, "Pour me another cup of coffee, Sugar. We've got business to attend to here."

Mr. Powell's newsletter is in the form of a photo-copied broadside from a New Smyrna Beach, Florida, address. "We have had many calls and letters," the newsletter reads, "from people owning land in River Ranch Acres who have attempted to visit their land and were turned away, harassed, or were told they would have to pay a fee to go through the gate to see their property." A so-called hunt club, constituted under the name River Ranch Property Owners Hunting Association, is claiming to have "full operation over the entire River Ranch Acres property."

Where the Hunt Club has derived authority to take over the 44,000 acres remains a mystery, since the members themselves have never owned more than a fraction of them. But somehow they've managed to lease the entire acreage to cattle ranchers, pocket the money, and build their hunting camps and vacation homes on whoever's property they want to. The armed guards posted at the main gate, the hunters say in their own newsletter, are for the "betterment, protection, organization, and coordination of the activities at River Ranch." If you are a landowner and can show the armed guards a copy of your deed and current paid tax bill, they say they will be "happy to escort you on a tour."

Dick Powell's newsletter contained photos indicating that these hunters and other squatters had moved onto the land in great numbers, erecting shacks, trailers, and even second homes illegally on landowners' property. It set my father's blood to boil.

Dad's coffee ritual was a sight to behold, particularly when he was thinking about armed squatters on his property. He poured an indeterminable amount of sugar and Pet evaporated milk into his cup and stirred vigorously until the coffee sloshed onto its saucer. He'd lift his steaming cup, blow across it a few times to cool it off enough for him to swallow the whole thing in two or three gulps, and then raise the saucer to his lips and slurp down the remainder with something akin to vengeance.

"More coffee, Sugar," he'd smile, and then turn back to me with a mock-serious look. "'Tain't funny, McGee," he'd say, a line from his favorite radio show, and then he'd get set for battle again.

"They're putting up tin trailers and outhouses and no telling what else on our land," he'd say. "They've got armed guards. You can't get in unless you pay them, and even then, you can't do anything with your land except look at it, but of course you can't find it because the thugs at the gate won't even let the surveyors in!"

Yeah, it looked bad, I thought. But at least it was something to talk about. We'd exhausted all our political arguments. I'd come to see, in my mid-thirties, that Dad had been pretty much right all along. And it was of no use for him to complain about my mother, because she was standing there tending the coffeepot, a living tragedy now, a half-blind visual artist, and Dad was seventy-two years old and not about, at this late date, to leave her, even if he had ever seriously considered it. Plus, now that I'd sobered up, I wasn't baiting Dad anymore about anything.

The time for the long heart-to-heart talks when he'd take me outside and we'd walk in the gardenia-scented air of his yard and he'd advise me about what to do in difficult situations and assure me that I was capable of overcoming any obstacle—those days seemed now to be at an end. I was going to be a father soon myself.

But there was always the topic of River Ranch. It was even better than talking about how the General Board of the Methodist Church was aiding Marxist guerrillas around the world and trying to take God the Father out of the hymnals and even the Bible! It was better than talking about the prices in the grocery stores, which were scandalous and demanded immediate attention on somebody's part. No, those two and a half acres at River Ranch had been Dad's only investment, and he would be hog-tied rather than see his land stolen by squatters and hired gunslingers.

"I think they ought to shoot 'em," he'd say, although he'd never owned a gun himself, and it was unclear who "they" were—the Polk County sheriff's department, some of whom were members of the Hunt Club, or federal law enforcement officials (Dad would rather die than see the federal government brought into this), or members of the Landowners Association like himself, most of whom were by now in their seventies or eighties and unlikely to be very good shots.

In 1983 my wife, Vicki, and I started taking Mom and Dad with us for a few days' vacation in Florida every year, not to Laguna Beach but a little farther west to Seagrove, on the highest point overlooking the Gulf of Mexico. It was thrilling, poignant, and a little scary to see my father bounding down the stairs and running across the beach and diving into the Gulf, just as he'd done on those family vacations thirty years before. The summer after our first child, Ashley, was born in 1985, we took Mom and Dad on their last trip to Florida. Dad couldn't make it down the stairs to the beach by this time. But he bottle-fed Ashley while Vicki and I took walks on the beach, and when his granddaughter fell asleep, Dad stood on the balcony alongside our golden retriever, Annie, and watched the ocean spread out before him in alternate bands of blue and green.

In these last years, Dad also revived an old tradition. He would take me to the nearby town of Freeport to buy fresh shrimp for the family's weekly shrimp boil. The 1950s had been our time for manly discussions about personal matters, things he never talked about with anyone else, including, I think, my mother, because they were usually about her—apologies for her inability to express love to us, her children; regrets about the life he'd fallen into with her; but hopes, too, about the future for all of us. On this last trip to Florida, we made our customary journey to Freeport. I drove, though. And Dad wanted to get some things settled.

"To my knowledge," he said, "no Covington has ever left anything to anybody." And then he smiled. "I don't intend to be the first."

It was his way, I think, of acknowledging the obvious: He was dying, and he didn't want me to take it too seriously. When we returned to Birmingham, he still derived pleasure from a cup of coffee over the morning paper, but his life by then had become more and more desiccated. He was bound to his oxygen tank in a house Mother kept at eighty degrees to save money on air-conditioning bills. His vertebrae had begun to collapse onto one another—an excruciating condition, but Mother had taken to hiding his pain pills. She was afraid in these last months of his life that he would become addicted to them. The only time I think he was the least bit comfortable was before dawn, when he would awaken before Mother and roll his oxygen tank to the front porch in order to watch Venus appear. It was cool out there in the morning, he told me, and the single planet was just lovely in the lightening sky.

Dad's last forays out into the world were about practical matters. Without telling us what he was up to, he somehow drove himself to the local funeral home and met with the director. Dad wanted the man to know that thirty years ago he had bought a burial policy for $50 and he expected only and exactly what was in the policy. He didn't want the director bugging his family about higher-priced caskets or a larger viewing room.

"Just give me what the policy covers," he said, "nothing more and nothing less."

My father died on April 21, 1988, at age seventy-six, in Birmingham, Alabama. He had always believed that dishonesty among men was an aberration in nature, like child pornography or a woman who worked outside the home. Although he had appeared once in debtors' court during the Great Depression, he had never defaulted on a loan or been charged with a crime. He was scrupulously honest about his income tax preparations. He did not like to bargain for anything, especially used cars. "Just tell me the price, and if I want it, I'll buy it," he'd say. He did not sue when a drunken Amway salesman crossed the center line of First Avenue North in East Lake and crashed head-on into Dad's VW, giving Mother superficial cuts and bruises and Dad an ankle fractured in a zillion places, so that the next Beetle he bought, light blue just like the first one, had to be an automatic, since Dad could no longer engage the clutch with his left foot.

Dad's insurance company did collect $10,000 from the other man's insurance company, but Dad divided that money into four parts and gave one portion to each of his four children.

My father never made more than $14,000 in any single year. The only true vacations he took were to Laguna Beach, Florida, and Gatlinburg, Tennessee. He never rode in a commercial airliner. He loved movie westerns, but the farthest west he got was east Texas. In his early fifties, though, at a time when it seemed he should be most disheartened by life, Dad bought that small parcel of River Ranch land in what was billed as a Western-styled subdivision in central Florida.

It was what he left me when he died.

In fact, the last trip my father made away from his house (other than the final ambulance ride to the hospital) was to a local bank so a notary public could sign and seal the deed transferring ownership of those two and a half acres in Florida to me. After his death, my sister and brothers and I joked about my inheritance— that deed to a worthless piece of land. But I believe Dad knew exactly what he was doing. I think he wanted me to have an adventure on his behalf. It was one of the enduring themes of the westerns he'd loved to watch—the reclaiming of family land that had been stolen by gunslingers and cattle barons—and I think he must have smiled inwardly with the thought that I might ride into Polk County, Florida, one day demanding justice, even if it meant riding into an ambush. *Gunfight at the O.K. Corral* was more than entertainment to my father. It represented the defense of a code, without which the west, and therefore the future, could never be fully civilized. Dad's outlook for America and the world at large had been grim before he died. "It's too late for me to change anything," he said the final time he voted. "I'll just vote for dictatorship and slavery." (He had intended to vote a straight Republican ticket that year, but accidentally pulled the lever for the Libertarian Party instead.)

But there was one dream of his that I thought could be salvaged, if only I could be as crazy in the defense of my inheritance as he had been in buying it, and then leaving it to me.

Access Points

In May of 1996, I bought a Jeep Cherokee with 219,000 miles on it and talked one of my nephews, Jeanie's son Craig, into riding with me to River Ranch to claim my inheritance. Craig was the perfect choice to ride shotgun—a a six-foot-two-inch former closed-head-injury patient who dipped snuff; loved jazz; spoke in brief, ironic understatement; and always had his brows knit as though he were considering grave and tragic consequences for anyone who looked at him or me the wrong way.

A few years earlier, Craig had been thrown through the windshield of a friend's car when the driver lost control. Somehow Craig had managed to ride the hood, gripping the dash while the car rolled three times down an embankment and into a line of trees—the source of his irony, I think. He was in a coma for about three weeks, and when he finally came out of it, the first thing he said was, "Anybody got a Little Debbie cake on them?"

By the time of our trip to Florida, Craig had recovered enough from the accident to know he hadn't completely recovered yet—he was still experiencing a minor dislocation in time and space. He would get lost on the most familiar of streets back home. And his days and nights would unexpectedly reverse. The *Tonight Show* would be on at what he thought was noon, for instance, and that would really piss him off.

"I don't blame God," he said to me on the way to River Ranch. "I just wish I knew what He was up to sometimes."

It was a fine day for travel, but the Jeep broke down after seven hours on the road, in Bainbridge, Georgia, a town with the largest high school football stadium I have ever seen. We had the Jeep towed off the interstate to a repair shop—nothing serious, just an alternator gone bad—and I watched while Craig thumbed a magazine in the customer service area and expertly spit snuff into an empty Mountain Dew bottle, the twenty-ounce size.

Back on the interstate, we listened to jazz on radio stations that Craig had an uncanny ability to find—Coltrane, Miles Davis, Zoot Sims. We talked about heat lightning and other anomalies—black holes, chaos theory, the capricious behavior of tornadoes. I asked him if he knew anything about holograms, and he said he'd seen them at Disney World, where three-dimensional ghosts were programmed to rise out of the shadows in a haunted house. I said I didn't know he'd gone to Disney World, and he reminded me that a number of years ago my mother and father had taken him and his sister, Judy, and their cousin Michael to Orlando.

"We stopped at River Ranch on the way back."

"You're kidding," I said. But it did ring a bell.

"Granddad Covington was crazy to show us his Florida property. Of course, he didn't know exactly where it was. We stayed at the River Ranch Resort. It kind of gave me the heebie-jeebies. I mean, it was a nice place, but there weren't any people around. It felt like a horror movie set."

Since that long-ago trip, Craig's cousin Michael had died—automobile accident at the age of twenty-five. My father died soon after that. And then my brother Scotty, Michael's own father, was killed in a freak industrial mishap.

So inevitably the discussion came around to death.

"The only thing I remember," Craig said, "was riding on the hood of that car and holding onto the dashboard while it flipped a few times. 'This is wild,' I thought. Next thing I know, I'm looking up out of a hospital bed into Judy's face. Not only do I not want to die. I don't *ever* want to get that close again."

I asked him if he was nervous about this trip to River Ranch, the Hunt Club and all that.

"Nah," he said, and I realized that the notion of having him ride shotgun had not been a joke. I really might

need Craig for protection. Even as I thought this, I was
saying to myself, "These are the kind of thoughts old
men think."

It is not a comfortable feeling, that peculiar vulnerabil-
ity that comes with age. You suddenly see yourself as
fragile inside, like the discarded exoskeleton of some
spiny sea creature. You are brittle where you once were
strong, soft where you once were resilient. Even if you
were never a real match for anyone in a physical contest,
you now feel as though not even courage or adrenaline
could keep you alive in a fight, even if you faced someone only half your size. This frame of mind might be
called despair, I think, except for the complementary
calm that comes with the knowledge that you are safe in
someone else's hands, the way you were when you were
a kid. Crossing the threshold of late middle age, you begin to feel defenseless, but until you really are defenseless, I don't believe you can understand the strength that
lies all around you, in family, community, friends. And
sailing through that Florida night, I was at peace know-
ing that no matter how badly I screwed things up at
River Ranch, Craig would be there.

The interstate south from the state line seemed endless. The same signs loomed out of the darkness in the
same sequence—signs advertising tourist maps, discount
motel coupons, Indian River grapefruit, and X-rated
cafes for couples only. Or maybe it was only one cafe
that was being advertised over and over again. And why

a cafe? Craig and I had a time trying to figure that one out.

We decided we'd been on the road too long, so we stayed the night at a Holiday Inn in Ocala, and the next morning we got off the interstate and took Highway 27 into a different Florida from the one I'd known as a boy. This Florida had a Mediterranean feel. The hills were rolling and quilted with groves of orange trees. Horses nibbled in pastures along the streambeds. The frogs were brown instead of green. And the sun seemed to come in at a more acute angle before reflecting off distant bell towers and red-tiled roofs.

I remembered that Mom and Dad and I must have cut across the state near here on that educational Florida trip to St. Augustine, and I tried to imagine Dad seeing this country for the first time and thinking of it as his. Dad himself had looked Mediterranean as a young man. In photos from the 1930s, he had an aquiline nose, black hair, and olive skin. Although Ashley assures me our ancestors were Anglo-Irish, we both have a feeling Dad's line must have crossed that of a darker race—perhaps the *melungeons,* those Spanish Jews (according to one legend) who had sailed to the New World with Hernando de Soto, explored the Tennessee River basin, and wound up on a hilltop in the northern part of the state. The lost tribe of Israel, some people say. What if one of their descendants, in a fire-engine red '59 Chevy Impala, had crossed central Florida on his way to St.

Augustine and seen orange groves for the first time, framed by shimmering minarets?

Would he have known they were oranges, since he was color-blind?

My vision of Dad as a Spanish Jew lasted only until the highway wound back into a more commercial and familiar Florida: strawberry stands, used-car lots, and acres of concrete deer statuary.

Lake Wales, the closest town of any size to River Ranch, was the home of Donald Duck orange juice and Floridino's Pizza and Pasta, in addition to The Singing Tower, whatever that might have been. After Lake Wales, it was flat prairie and pine thickets all the way to the horizon. We knew we were approaching River Ranch when we saw the neon sign of the Indian Lake Motel on our right; the intersection of Highways 60 and 630 dead ahead; and a sign for Yeehaw Junction, an unfortunately named crossroads between River Ranch and the backwater town of Okeechobee. The police chief in Okeechobee, I had read somewhere, was a member of the Hunt Club—as was a game warden named Wee-Wee and a number of sheriff's deputies and other keepers of the public trust.

We pulled to a stop and got out. The original Hunt Club gatehouse had been located here, off Highway 60 just west of the intersection. I recognized the site from photos in Dad's old newsletters. There was nothing now to suggest human interest in the place except for a couple of discarded tires and an unimproved, sandy track that ended at a barbed-wire fence with a gate that looked to be wrapped in locks and chains, like the ghost of Christmas past.

I consulted my topographical map. Armed with a protractor and the legal description, I'd located Dad's land on the map and penciled it in, a small green square that was miles from either of the highways but looked to be brushed at one corner by a dirt road. Late at night in Birmingham, I had stared at that tiny square, wondering if that road crossed the property line. I was trying to decide where a cabin might be erected, a well drilled, a garden planted.

"This is where we're standing," I told Craig as I pointed to the map. "And here's Dad's land."

"So where's the Hunt Club?" he asked.

I looked up. The sun was low now, throwing the shadows of pines across the Jeep's hood. "About two hundred yards up thataway," I said, and I pointed down Highway 630 toward the southwest. Behind me, the sky was already darkening into dusk.

I don't know what I'd expected, but the Hunt Club's gatehouse, a frame building shaded by trees, appeared more substantial than necessary to oversee the raising and lowering of a simple gate. It was, in fact, a home for the gatekeeper and his wife and a mingling point for hunters looking to swap tales or make phone calls or post notices or simply rest their feet. The enclosed porch served as a common area. Behind the counter were the living quarters, off-limits to anybody but the most senior higher-ups.

The gatekeeper, Mac McQueen, was snapping beans when we arrived. He had thick, callused hands, a shock of white hair, and a revolver strapped to his waist. "You're a long way from home," he said. "Don't they have enough deer up there in Alabama to suit you?"

Mac's wife, Thelma, was more direct. "What are you doing down here?" she asked. She was standing at the counter underneath a calendar advertising deer stands and camouflage vests. She had narrow eyes and a crooked smile. The static from a CB radio crackled behind her.

"I just wanted to show my nephew our land."

"What section is it in?" Mac asked.

I told him.

"That land is worthless," he said without looking up from his beans. "You can't camp on it. You can't do anything on it, unless you want a thirty-aught-six going through you."

(A thirty-aught-six is a round from a high-powered rifle that blasts an exit hole in your back the size of a man's fist.)

Craig and I conferred in front of the nearby Coke machine while the woman in line behind us, a soccer mom whose kids were still in the sport utility with Michigan tags, inquired about overnight camping.

"Are you a member of the club?" Mac asked.

"This is River Ranch, isn't it?"

He stared at her. "You must be looking for the River Ranch Resort."

"I'm on my way to Key West. We're camping. We have a tent."

"This isn't a campground," Mac said. "This is private property."

"My family owns land here." The woman glanced at me. Mac glanced at me. I glanced at them both. Thelma took the beans into the kitchen to boil.

"I wouldn't camp here if I were you," Mac said. "There are alligators and wild hogs everywhere. Rattlesnakes, too. I wouldn't take my children anyplace like that."

The woman carefully unfolded her deed and showed it to him. He stroked his stubbled gray chin as though he were deciphering fine print. The mosquitoes were coming out, I noticed, mosquitoes as big as fruit bats, and they wobbled toward the yellow outdoor light that Thelma had just turned on.

Thelma reappeared behind the counter and craned to look over Mac's shoulder. "You must be one of those people that got hoodwinked," she said to the woman from Michigan. "That land company just told a whole bunch of lies. You may have a deed, but you can't go into the hunting area or the common areas. You can't four-wheel it. You can't use the roads or trash receptacles."

"I'll take my chances," the woman said in a crisp Northern accent I liked.

"Well, I'll have to see your tax receipt or canceled check," Mac said.

"Come again?"

"I've got to have proof you paid this year's property taxes. It's Hunt Club rules. If you're not a member and you come in on a deed, you've got to show proof your taxes are paid up and current. Otherwise, how do we know you still own the land?"

Silence hung for a moment.

"Who do you think you are?" the woman finally said. Her mouth was set in a hard, hooked line. She took back her deed from Mac and turned to leave. Before she did, she caught my eye again, and I knew what she was thinking: that I was one of them.

I wanted to set the Michigan woman straight, but she was out of the gatehouse before I could marshal my words. We heard the SUV door slam and the angry sound of tires on gravel as she pulled away toward the highway and Key West.

The gatehouse was stifling. I rummaged through my backpack and then handed Mac a copy of Dad's deed, the notarized transfer signed by two witnesses, and a canceled check for that year's property taxes, which had come to $21.56. Mac perused these documents, reluctantly told me to sign in, and then motioned for Thelma to open the gate.

"You better be out of there by dark."

The sign beside the gate read, ALL PERSON WHO ENTER DO SO AT THEIR OWN RISK.

Inside at last, Craig and I took a look around. This part of River Ranch was a landscape of beat-up tin shacks with dog runs and outhouses; junked appliances and swamp buggies loomed beneath the trees like the intact skeletons of steel dinosaurs. The buggies' tires alone were four or five feet high. Airplane tires, I thought. And the jerry-rigged chassis, with platforms for hunters to stand on and fire, effectively doubled the height. One of the swamp buggies was plastered with Confederate flag decals. Another sported the sign "If you can't run with the big dogs, stay on the porch."

The camps themselves had names like "Camp Run-a-Muck," "Hawg Heaven," and "Leisure Village at Armadillo Bay." An oily sheen floated on the surface of the water in the potholes, and the air was foul with the smell of diesel and spent cordite. The Hunt Club was having a turkey shoot that day to raise money for a new hog pen; the last shots echoed flatly across the palmetto fields.

We drove through the sand and muck for a couple of miles until the road petered out in a brackish lake. Braided buggy trails ran off at chaotic angles into the palmetto on either side, and a hand-painted sign was posted on a nearby pine. "Confusion Corner," it read.

I told Craig that one of those trails was probably the one that led to Dad's land, but I didn't know which, and I wasn't sure the Jeep could handle the water in the lake despite Craig's opinion that it could. I'd never driven off-road before. In short, I chickened out. I turned the

Jeep around and headed back toward the Hunt Club gate. The sky had turned yellow, with bands of orange and magenta clouds, and then it fell into the dark, brooding blue of a prairie night. Our headlights suddenly lit on the spoils of a hunt. The buck, a spike, had been field-dressed and lashed across the front of a swamp buggy, its eyes starting to cloud, its belly slit open and the edges oozing thick, black blood. We nodded at the two hunters who were pissing against the swamp buggy's tires.

"Nice inheritance," Craig said.

I soon discovered that it wasn't going to be easy to get Dad's land surveyed. Thumbing through the yellow pages, I found a surveyor who said he'd do it for $2,000, but he strongly advised against it. "You know, the Hunt Club doesn't want any surveying done out there. They'll do just about anything to keep people out."

I told him that's what I'd gathered.

But then I ran across Bill Read, the man who had done the original survey of River Ranch for Gulf American. He said he'd have one of his crews survey Dad's land for $700. "I'll go out myself if I have to," he said. "That bunch of rednecks doesn't scare me."

Mr. Read was in his early seventies, lean and blue-eyed, with a military bearing and gray flattop—a former Navy man. He said he had come from a family of English bell-ringers, some of whom were visiting him and his wife that very weekend. "They're a pretty rowdy crowd," he said.

I was at Mr. Read's sun-filled office in Bartow, the county seat, having left Craig at the River Ranch Resort, where we were the only guests. Phone service to the resort had been cut off that morning for nonpayment. The maids told us their most recent paychecks had bounced. The resort was no longer a part of the River Ranch subdivision, but there was nonetheless a whiff of disaster in the air.

Mr. Read unrolled a huge plat map onto the table. "If they'd actually developed River Ranch the way I'd drawn it on paper, it would have looked like New York City out there," he said.

The place names on the map were familiar— Rattlesnake Hammock, Dead Pecker Slough. But the land itself was covered by the intricate pattern of what appeared to be an enormous residential subdivision, complete with dashes for road rights-of-way.

"These lots don't exist on the ground," Mr. Read said. "I just laid a grid right on top of the map. I never surveyed the lots, never surveyed anything smaller than a 640-acre section. It was a conspiracy from the start."

I asked him what he meant by conspiracy.

"You might not want to say I told you this," he said. And then he described the pivotal meeting between Polk County commissioners and representatives of Gulf American at John's Restaurant in Bartow more than thirty years before, when Gulf American had assured county officials that they would never have to maintain any roads because there wouldn't be any. Gulf American had its way, and since that meeting, the county had raked in millions in River Ranch property taxes.

"It was in the best interest of both parties," Mr. Read concluded. "The ones who suffered were the buyers who took the bait."

"Like my dad."

He nodded.

I asked him how I could get to the land without having to go through the Hunt Club's gate.

"The old gate used to be here," he said and pointed at the spot near the intersection of Highways 60 and 630 where Craig and I had stood the day before. "The Hunt Club people moved it when someone reminded them that they didn't own the land the gate was on. So they bought eleven acres up here." And he pointed to the spot where the gatehouse now stood.

"But here's the thing," he said. "The parcel they bought wasn't part of River Ranch Acres. It belonged to another subdivision called Sunhill Estates, which was owned by some South American individuals who built a landing strip there. But that's another story."

I told him he'd lost me.

"The Hunt Club's gate isn't a legal access point to River Ranch."

"So who owns the fence?" I asked.

He said the Hunt Club members acted like they did, but they didn't. Some people thought the fence belonged to one of the cattle ranchers who leased rangeland from the Hunt Club, even though the club didn't own that, either. The fence actually belonged to an Australian named John Kennelly, who had bought more than 10,000 acres of River Ranch from Avatar, the holding company that had taken over after GAC went bankrupt.

"The easements are recorded in favor of the property owners and the general public," Mr. Read said, "but the Hunt Club controls the only unlocked gate."

I don't remember Mr. Read's exact words at this point, but his meaning was sufficiently clear: Armed men were patrolling a fence that wasn't theirs, in order to keep intruders off land that wasn't theirs, so that they could charge their members and guests thousands of dollars to use a gate that wasn't even a legal access point to the land in the first place.

I asked Mr. Read how he was going to get to Dad's parcel in order to survey it.

"They won't touch me," he said. "They know who I am. But it'd be different for you."

I asked him what I should do.

"Be careful when you're out there," he said. "And talk to Dick Powell. He's been trying for years to get the courts to open up access points to River Ranch. If it was me," he added, leaning close, "I'd cut the fence."

"The Hunt Club's just a bunch of outlaws chewing tobacco and shooting up the world," Dick Powell told Craig and me at his office in New Smyrna

Beach the next day. "I've cut the wire dozens of times. I've never gone through their gate."

Powell was president of the River Ranch Landowners Association and author of the newsletters whose articles had so inflamed my father before he died. His office was spartan, but filled with maps and aerial photos of River Ranch. He also had a hand grenade in his in-box and an M-31 grenade rifle by his computer. "Just souvenirs," he explained. He said he had received numerous death threats from members of the Hunt Club. They had also sent him packages of human excrement through the mail. "And it's not just me," he said. "When the vice-president of a Fortune 500 outfit tried to visit his company's property, they threatened to kill his children."

Craig and I must have looked a little stunned.

"I think I'll take a walk to the beach and let you two talk," Craig said. He was lifting himself out of his chair.

"It's a beautiful beach," Powell said. "Don't pay any attention to what they say about sharks. There hasn't been an attack in weeks."

In the lull after Craig left, I tried to take stock of Dick Powell. He appeared to be in his early fifties, a handsome guy with a dark mustache, sturdy—almost corpulent—and dressed (as was his custom, I'd later find out) in black. To hear Powell tell it, his life had been pointed all along toward political and legal battles just like this one. After high school and a stint as an electronics technician in the Army, he had worked for Southern Bell and later AT&T, retiring in 1990 with thirty years of service.

For much of that time he had also been president of the Communication Workers of America local. "I cut my teeth fighting problems here in Volusia County," he said. "I was usually able to subdue them with pretty simple court work and injunctions."

But River Ranch was a different matter. His grandmother left a piece of it to family members. After being alerted by people who owned land in the subdivision but couldn't get in to see it, Powell bought the parcel himself and founded the River Ranch Landowners Association in 1981. "I was told if I went in, I would probably not be able to walk back out. It's been a battle ever since."

For years, Powell tried to pursue a class-action suit against the Hunt Club, but he could never get past the initial hurdle of establishing the existence of an aggrieved class of plaintiffs, for he was probably the only association member who had managed to get his land surveyed.

The flash point came after one of his appeals on behalf of the association had been remanded, with prejudice, back to a lower court and then dismissed. In a calculated rage, Powell decided to act in his self-interest. To gain access to his land, he applied for, and was granted, a driveway permit from the state of Florida. Then, starting near the intersection of Highways 630 and 60, he bulldozed a road right through the barbed-wire fence and up a section line to his property. That night, the Hunt Club simply erected another fence, this one across Powell's driveway, and this time the fence posts were telephone poles set in concrete.

So Powell showed up one day with wire cutters and a state highway patrolman who was there to protect him while he walked up the state-approved driveway to his land. Unfortunately, members of the Hunt Club also showed up, along with Polk County sheriff's deputy Gene Smith. A scuffle ensued in which Hunt Club members shoved Powell and punched a guy videotaping the proceedings. The law officers broke up the fracas, but then sheriff's deputy Smith made a startling announcement: He would arrest anybody who attempted to cut the barbed-wire fence.

Perplexed, the highway patrolman radioed his superior, who advised him to leave the area immediately, since there were "political ramifications." It had been the State of Florida versus Polk County, and it appeared the county had won.

I later asked deputy Smith, under the gaze of a stuffed boar's head hanging on the wall at the sheriff's office, how the Hunt Club could get away with charging people to enter River Ranch Acres through a gate that wasn't a legal access point. He said, "You're right about that. The Hunt Club gate is not a legal access point to River Ranch Acres. It's an *egress* point. In other words, the Hunt Club is just letting people who are already in River Ranch get out through their gate."

Dick Powell had his own interpretation. "Gene Smith is a real stupid idiot," he said.

On the advice of a new attorney, Powell intended to ask the court for a declaratory judgment affirming the validity of the easements to his property. (Only the Hunt Club and the sheriff's department, he said, were maintaining that they weren't valid.) With that one small victory in hand, Powell could petition a judge to order that the fence come down. But he had no illusions about the cost or difficulty of the process.

He pointed out that the Hunt Club's attorney was president of the Florida Bar Association and a close friend of the governor, who happened to be from Polk County himself. "The county employees are so involved in this, they have to protect each other no matter what," Powell said.

River Ranch was their private playground, he added, but nobody did much hunting there. "No self-respecting deer would hang around with twelve-foot-high swamp buggies roaring by." What really went on at River Ranch, Powell said, was gambling, prostitution, illegal liquor sales, and marijuana cultivation.

"They've got a whorehouse out there called the Doe Camp," he said. "It's a bunch of trailers set up with the women in them. During hunting season, you can get you a woman by calling a guy named Rooster on your CB. If you need whiskey, you just call a guy named The Tanker. Friday, Saturday nights, it's a big orgy out there."

Suddenly a thought seemed to seize him. "There's a character out there you might be interested in, a marijuana farmer of some consequence. He's related to somebody high up in the Hunt Club, and he lives in a tin shack on the edge of a hammock. He's filthy, stinks, reeks of urine. Maybe you could run into him and be-friend him." He smiled. "You're a writer. You two might get along."

"This is starting to give me the willies," Craig said when we left New Smyrna Beach. "Remember when that guy at the gatehouse said you couldn't camp on your property unless you wanted a thirty-ought-six go-ing through you?"

I nodded.

"That was a funny way to put it."

Craig had a point, but I told him I thought Mac was referring to hunters mistaking us for deer or hogs.

"That's not how I took it," Craig said.

In truth, it wasn't the way I had taken it, either.

"Are you going to join the Landowners Association?" Craig asked.

I told him, no, I was going to join the Hunt Club.

"Good idea," he said, deadpan.

Crackers

The annual general meeting of the Hunt Club was held that February at the old Frostproof High School auditorium. It had peeling walls and faded yellow curtains. There were about 120 of us there. I'd made an effort to look like the other members, not a hard thing to do, after all. We dressed pretty much alike. I'd never seen so many flannel shirts and dirty ball caps in one place at the same time. The one concession I made was to cut my hair a little shorter than usual. I didn't want to have to wear it in a mullet, and the impression I'd gotten was that long hair was tolerated only in that particularly gruesome style.

I told the girls when I'd joined the club, on the morning of the July 4th pig roast, that they might need to act a little redneck.

"Come on, Dad," Ashley said.

But then a woman in the pickup beside us slapped her daughter's leg and said, "Get your stink butt off my cooler. You done spilt candy all over the place."

"I see what you mean," Laura whispered to me.

Vicki and the girls had been kind enough to play along with me then, but I didn't want to implicate them any further in this ruse. Besides, I knew I finally couldn't misrepresent myself to the hunters. I told the first one I talked to that I was a writer, and I'm sure that bit of information hit the CB airwaves overnight.

Later, I asked Pete Edwards, the club president, if I could go hog hunting with him, or if he knew anybody who might let me tag along. I see now what an odd question that must have been. "No, I don't know anybody here who'd do that," he said. "There's a guy way down in South Florida, though. You could give him a call."

So, after I found my seat in the auditorium, I didn't try to hide the fact that I was taking notes. I couldn't even claim to be a journalist. Objectivity wasn't in the cards. I had an ax to grind with the Hunt Club, and sooner or later, the other members would find out.

The club treasurer was reporting that he had bought 357 hogs at $20 a head. He and Billy Fitzpatrick had turned them out, he said, and as of that date, ninety-seven hogs had been killed. "I knowed there's more killed than that," said Pete Edwards. "I knowed one man killed seven."

The other officers, seated at a long table up-center, seemed to shrink as Mr. Pete, as they called their outgoing president, strode to the microphone. He was a big man, white-headed and resplendent in a gray Stetson and cowboy boots. His enormous silver belt buckle flashed in the auditorium lights when he shifted his weight from one foot to the other. He adjusted the microphone, took a long look at the membership, and smiled approvingly at what he saw. "Yeah, I know about you, Swamp Buster," he said to someone in the front row, and a ripple of laughter moved through the ball caps that surrounded the man. Then, after commenting on the success of the lighted Christmas Swamp Buggy Parade, a festive event enjoyed by all, Mr. Pete said he wanted to update us on some other old business.

"Powell's been giving us hell," he said, "but this time we've got him stopped."

There was a sustained burst of applause, punctuated by shouts of relief and encouragement. "They can't cross our property on that section line!" Pete shouted. "Powell thought he'd bought it, but he hadn't!"

Each time he said the name, he pronounced it "Pile," and each time, the word seemed more acidic and vile.

Mr. Pete waited until the auditorium settled down and then continued more matter-of-factly. "Pile's got six acres in there, and he tried to bulldoze a road up the section line to get to them. Problem is, he didn't own the access point on the highway. So he went and bought one and a quarter acres on the highway, or thought he did."

Billy Fitzpatrick, the vice-president, slapped his thigh and grinned at the other officers.

"Trouble is, the owner hadn't paid his taxes in a while," Pete said.

"Y'all remember to pay your taxes," Billy Fitzpatrick interjected. "I don't care whether you're on the deed with a dozen of your friends and not a one of you knows where the land is at, you've got to pay those taxes."

"Anyway, this owner hadn't," Pete continued. "He was probably from up north. So when I got wind of what Pile was up to, I went to the courthouse first thing in the morning and bought that one and a quarter acres right out from under him for back taxes. You know, a tax deed takes precedence over the other kind."

Then Mr. Pete explained how Powell was trying to get in court what he couldn't get any other way. "The suit's against me and my wife and the cattlemen who own the fence. The club has already paid a $5,000 retainer."

At that moment, a member with curly hair and glasses, a bird hunter from the looks of him, spoke up from the audience. "If all Powell's got is six acres, why spend all that money fighting him about it?"

Pete looked down at the man as though just now sniffing something unpleasant. "I bought that property to stop him from coming in."

"Why you?" the bird hunter asked. "Why don't we pay to defend our people on the other section lines?"

Alan Ingram, the bearded young man who was Pete's choice to replace him as president, stepped to the microphone and took over the answer. "Powell's suing for access across that property to open up a road. If Powell opens that road, anybody can come in."

Pete tilted the microphone in his own direction again. "Why should I reach into my own pocket to pay a five- or six- or ten-thousand-dollar lawyer bill to keep somebody from coming across my $600 property?" he asked. "It's the club's obligation to keep Pile from coming across my land."

By now, Pete's face had turned beet red. He was knifing the edge of one of his big hands into the palm of the other to emphasize his points. "I didn't have five or six thousand dollars in my wallet at the time. And if I had, I still wouldn't have paid it. It was in the club's interest to pay that lawyer's fee. So the club paid it."

This time it was Billy Fitzpatrick who took the microphone. "I think everybody knows what Pete Edwards has done for this club—"

But Pete wasn't finished yet, and he didn't need a microphone. "I hope we've got Pile stopped," he said as he paced the stage. "Because if we don't, there won't be no club. Do you hear what I'm saying? If you let one landowner in, you've got to let all of them in," Pete said, "and that would be the end of the club!" He paused to allow the magnitude of that disaster to sink in.

"I hear there's other property involved," said the bird hunter. "What are we doing spending our money to buy this other property on the highway?"

Pete stiffened. "I talked the board into buying that property because there's a man wants to put a gun and knife shop on it. But don't worry," he said. "The gun shop owner assured me that if he ever saw Pile cross his land, he'd shoot the hell out of him!"

The auditorium erupted in whoops and applause, and the curly-haired bird hunter and his wife slipped out of the auditorium before the ruckus had even begun to die down.

When I later asked Alan Ingram, the incoming president, about the Hunt Club's armed guards, he said the club didn't have any. But on a day in the middle of the general gun season, my photographer friend Jim Neel and I walked into the gatehouse right after Bubba Fletcher, a local rancher, had called to say he'd been shot at. The Hunt Club sent two of its men to investigate. Both wore revolvers in holsters strapped to their waists, like characters in a spaghetti western.

"I'd just love to shoot somebody today!" one of the men said before he flung open the screen door and jumped into an idling truck that disappeared in a pall of exhaust.

I didn't recognize the woman behind the counter this time. She was younger than Thelma, tougher looking. She had a moon-shaped face, wore thick glasses, and was missing a couple of bottom front teeth. I'd find out her name was Sue, that one of the armed guards was her man, Steve, and that they lived in a camp called Shiloh not far inside the Hunt Club's gate. I'd seen the camp that morning. It had wash on the line, a blue-tick hound chained to a fence post, and a rusted Dodge up on blocks in the side yard.

"What happened to Mac and Thelma?" I asked.

"I don't think they could handle it here." Sue blew a smoke ring toward the ceiling. "It's bad enough for me and Steve. We already work twelve hours a day, and last night when the relief-shift guy got here, he was so drunk, all he could do was pass out on the couch."

My friend Jim asked what all the hubbub had been about, and Sue told us about Bubba Fletcher's call. "During hunting season, everybody's bound to have a story that somebody got shot at. We have one lady wrote a big long letter. Somebody supposedly fired into her trailer."

"Anybody hurt?" I asked.

Sue shook her head. "I think they just did it to make her mad. And break-ins happen all the time," she added. "On Friday, Saturday nights, people are bashing this person, that person. You're just gonna get that. I'm waiting for somebody to break into my trailer." She patted the nine-millimeter pistol that she kept in plain sight on the counter.

About that time, the CB behind her squawked. It was Steve and the other guard reporting that they couldn't find the person who had shot at Bubba Fletcher. Sue said she figured it was a hermit property owner who lived way back in the woods somewhere. "Nobody knows who he is or where he's going or where he's been to."

She said he'd been spotted a couple of times in the camping area, though, and some people were starting to get nervous. "Scared the living daylights out of one couple," she said. They reported the man was wearing camouflage. He had long hair and carried a high-powered rifle. People had started calling him "the camouflage man."

"A rumor starts," Sue said, "and before you know it, there's a crazy man running around in camouflage around here." She shook her head again and flicked cigarette ash into an empty Budweiser can. "But I can think of a couple of people this description fits. One person in particular comes to mind."

I asked her who that might be. I was thinking about the man Powell told me lived in a tin shack on a hammock way back in the woods, the marijuana farmer of some consequence, the guy who stank.

"I'm not spreading gossip," Sue said. "I wouldn't want Pete to get mad at me. I just . . . I think society's given this man a bad rap. He can't deal with the anxiety, the panic attack the city gives him." Then she looked directly at me. "Desperate men do desperate things."

Later that afternoon, we saw Steve skinning a wild hog, and Jim started taking photographs until Steve looked up from his bloody work and said, "I can tell you right now you're not taking any pictures of me."

"What if I shoot around you?" Jim said.

"I've been doing this since I was a kid," Steve said, "and there ain't no way you can get a picture of me skinning a hog without me being in it. I had enough of that in Vietnam."

So Jim put his camera away.

Whether a real or mythic figure, the camouflage man seemed to be an emblem of divisions within the Hunt Club itself, for the club was not a classless society. There were the hog hunters, and then there were the "camo hunters," and in between stood everybody else. The hog hunters' greatest fear was that the person or persons most likely to destroy the club would try to do it from the inside out. Their distrust of the stealthy bird and deer hunters seemed to coalesce around the legend of the camouflage man.

The first thing Hunt Club members will tell you, by the way, is that "Hunt Club" is not the name of their organization. The official name is River Ranch Property Owners Association, Inc.—not to be confused with Powell's group, the River Ranch Landowners Association. Members say the use of the term "Hunt Club" is "an attempt to downgrade" them. Hardly anyone, though, even among the members themselves, actually refers to the organization as anything other than the Hunt Club. It's a simple, straightforward name that accurately describes what most of the members say they do—hunt. But hunters are a notably diverse lot, differentiated by such incidental factors as age, sex, race, religion, and place of origin; and by two fundamental considerations: animal hunted and type of weapon used.

I have never seen a black man hunt anything at River Ranch Acres, for instance. This may have something to do with the unhappy history of the counties that make up central Florida. In the 1920s, this part of the state had a higher per capita incidence of lynchings than either Alabama or Mississippi. This may come as a surprise to residents of Boca Raton or Key Biscayne, but it will surprise no one at the closest bar to Indian Lake Estates, where Donna LeProux pours shots of Wild Turkey, chased with tepid beer, under a photograph of Buckwheat chowing down on a wedge of watermelon.

The area that now encompasses Polk County was settled in the 1700s by what one observer called "an improvident and lawless set of paupers from the frontiers of Virginia, Maryland, the Carolinas, and Georgia. . . . Generally gaunt, pale and leather-skinned, they appeared to know neither necessity nor desire, but only silent, joyless, painless existence, which is perfect in its way as a tree or a stone."

On the vast pine and palmetto prairies of central Florida, these immigrants had found a perfect spot to raise livestock, some of it their own. The Spaniards had brought cows and hogs whose descendants now wandered the open range. The new residents had only to hunt them down, brand them, and turn them back out into the wild. Thus was the Florida cattle industry born. Whenever a customer showed up to buy a cow, these

Florida cowmen would just hunt one up. They became known as "cow hunters," and the cows they hunted turned into a scrawny but tenacious breed that the artist Frederic Remington described as having bones that protruded so far "you could hang a hat on them."

People began calling the cow hunters "crackers" because of the sounds their rawhide whips made when snapped above the heads of cows. And the open range was crucial to the culture that grew up around this livelihood. Men could get killed for erecting fences, or cutting fences, either one. Even in the twentieth century, fence wars had taken the lives of prominent Polk County citizens. It is no wonder that Hunt Club members who were native to this part of the state had a volatile temper over issues of land ownership and use. These club members were more than likely hog hunters. The members from out-of-state or from the Atlantic or Gulf Coasts were more likely to be deer hunters or bird hunters. So the Hunt Club, despite being, like Polk County itself, predominantly white, was still divided along these class lines.

The deer and bird hunters sometimes referred to the hog hunters as "rednecks," "white trash," or just "jerks." The hog hunters most often referred to the other hunters as "shitheads."

I came from the same stock as the hog hunters, those poor whites from the Carolinas, but the only hunting I had ever done was to shoot at rabbits out of season from a speeding Ford convertible filled with restless teenage boys. We were supposed to be playing Ping Pong in the church basement, but our youth director had passed out .22-caliber rifles and taken us for a turn around the dirt roads near Ragland, Alabama, where I believe his grandmother lived. I think this youth director wanted to get fired. I took a number of shots and may even have spun a rabbit around. But my friend Lee Bryant insisted it was his shot that got the rabbit, and he sulked all the way back to Birmingham. I do remember putting a bullet hole through the floorboard of the convertible after we stopped for gas near Trussville. I was just checking to see whether the gun was loaded or not. It was.

That had been many years ago, and despite a stint in the Army, I still didn't know much about guns. But I knew enough to understand that the guns the hog hunters carried were not just for hunting hogs.

Despite this realization, I didn't bring a gun with me on my next trip to River Ranch. Instead, I brought a global positioning system (GPS) personal navigator. A GPS device is an extraordinary invention. Hand-held, battery-operated, and inexpensive, it can get a fix on satellites and, with the information beamed back, tell you exactly where you are on the surface of the earth. I have always needed such a device. A GPS can plot a course to a desired destination. It can point you the direction home when you're lost. It can calculate your speed, your progress, your estimated time of arrival. When it's in simulation mode, you can watch a map of the future, with you moving across it in a straight line toward your objective. It even has a "man overboard" feature. If you were in a boat in the middle of a lake, say, and happened to fall overboard, your companion with a GPS could immediately punch a button, and no matter how far the boat traveled before it stopped, he'd be able to find you by following the GPS's instructions on the screen.

I used aerial photographs, topo maps, and the GPS to locate Dad's land. I'd gone through dense thicket and mudholes whose water came over the hood of my Jeep. I'd seen rows of squatters' houses, some fastidiously neat, and some, like the camp belonging to a family called the Mirees, junked up with wrecked school buses and house trailers and foul-smelling garbage pits. I'd even seen a suspicious circle of pink trailers with a sign out front, the cut-out figure of a woman with enormous breasts and electrified hair. But the moment I left the thickets and trailers and junk piles behind, the land opened up all around me, and a bald eagle soared overhead. The sun was coming from behind, casting a veneer of light across the field. I was about four miles from the Hunt Club's main gate. There were no squatters' shacks, no sign of human habitation. It was exactly as I had imagined it—a vast palmetto plain, dotted with occasional pines. Dad's land was flat and beautiful in the way that only empty space itself is beautiful—the perfection being derived from what is not there.

Using the GPS, I found the approximate corners of his parcel. Then I set up a tent in the middle of the property and slept a long, sound sleep.

The next morning I went exploring. I was trying to find a way out of River Ranch that would avoid the Hunt Club's gate. What I found instead was another gate, locked and guarded by a stooped and disheveled old man with sparse white hair and a shotgun. One of his eyes was set in a perpetual squint. Whoever he was, he wasn't the camouflage man.

I wished the man a good morning, and he glared up at me with his good eye as though he already suspected I'd be trouble for him.

"I'm looking for the hawk that got one of my hens," he said. "I know it's illegal to shoot them, but what the hawk did was illegal, too. You with the government?"

I shook my head and told him I was from Alabama. I owned some property at River Ranch and wondered if I could cross his land to get back to Highway 60.

"The Hunt Club wouldn't like that," he said. "But you can come on in to my place. I got some black-eyed peas on the stove." He unlocked the gate, and I followed him down the rutted road toward his trailer. We passed a catfish pond, two cows, a brood of bantam chickens, and four pigs.

"My people are from Alabama, too," he ventured.

I sensed an opening and asked if I might have a key to his gate, so I wouldn't have to go all the way to the Hunt Club's gatehouse every time I wanted to get to or leave my property.

"Can't do that," he said. "I've given keys to the president of the Hunt Club, a couple of beekeepers who
come back here, the cow man, the game warden, and
the Polk County sheriff's department."

He leaned his shotgun against the trailer. "That's the
only ones allowed to use this gate. The rest have to pay
their fifty dollars and go through the Hunt Club."

I followed him up the steps into the trailer, which
smelled of black-eyed peas and pork rind and disinfec-
tant. The furnishings were sparse—an Easy Boy recliner
with the stuffing of the arms coming out, a black and
white TV on a pine table, two lawn chairs, a sink, a
fridge, and an electric range.

"Tell you the truth, I'm a little peeved that the Hunt
Club makes me pay $50 a year to go out hunting on
that land, especially since it's my road. I'm thinking
about not paying them this year."

He lifted the lid from the steaming pot of black-eyed
peas and stirred the froth with a wooden spoon. "Yep,"
he said. "They'll not get their fucking fifty out of me."

I stood and watched a little of the baseball game on
TV, the Braves at Pittsburgh, it appeared, but I couldn't
be sure, since the volume was turned completely down
and the picture was as grainy as the first shots from
America's landing on the moon. I think it was the bottom of the seventh inning when the man spooned up
two bowls of black-eyed peas, and we sat down to eat.

The black-eyed peas tasted like smoke. The man had
cut up some Vidalia onions and a fresh tomato. We also
had leftover cornbread and glasses of buttermilk to dip

the cornbread into, but we didn't make a production out of it. We just ate and talked mainly about Alabama. He said his people were from around Opelika and Dothan. They had lost the home place during the Great Depression and moved down to Bonifay, Florida, in the Panhandle. That's where he'd been born.

"Tolliver," he said. "Franklin Tolliver. That's my name. I got an aluminum recycling business up in Haines City. I just come down here to feed the animals and check on the place."

I asked him what else he knew about the Hunt Club, and he gave me a dismissive shrug. I guess he figured he'd told me enough already.

"What about the Doe Camp?" I asked.

Mr. Tolliver looked at me hard with his good eye. The bad one was crusted over and sunken in.

"How'd you hear about that?"

"Just rumors," I said.

Mr. Tolliver took his time clearing the table, as though he was turning something over in his head. He deposited the bowls and spoons into the sink with a clatter, filled the sink with hot water, and opened a window to let out the steam. It had been a cold, brisk morning, and I could see the air moving in the whorls at the back of his head.

"I could have bought all this shit for nothing when I first came down here," he said. "I'd heard about the women who worked in the canneries. Their husbands weren't giving them enough dick."

He waited, as if to gauge my reaction to that hopeful bit of news.

"I could have been rich," he continued. He added that he did, in fact, buy seventeen whorehouses and parcels of land, but he squandered almost all his money on the whores.

"Women using their pussy to pay the rent—that don't pay taxes," he said.

I nodded sympathetically.

"So if that's what you've got in mind, getting in with the Hunt Club and all them, just remember what happened to me."

"What's that?"

"I made a choice," Mr. Tolliver said. "I could have either made my fortune or had a good time." He looked more or less directly at me, but I couldn't tell which eye to look back into, the good one or the one that was bad.

"I had a good time," he said.

That afternoon, when I stopped at the gatehouse on the way out, another gatekeeper, a woman named Peanut, asked if that had been my tent and Jeep out there in the hunting area. She said if they were, the leadership of the Hunt Club wanted to talk to me.

"Anytime," I said.

"They're upset because you camped in the hunting area."

I shrugged.

"It can be dangerous out there," she said.

I reminded her that it wasn't even hunting season.

"That's not what I mean." Her watery blue eyes seemed filled with something like regret. "It's against the

Hunt Club rules to camp anywhere but the camping area."

I asked her who had decided what was the camping area and what was the hunting area.

"It's just a gentleman's agreement, I guess," she said.

I told her the land I'd camped on was mine.

"That may be," she said, "but the leaders of the Hunt Club can't guarantee your safety if you camp on it."

"Aw, come on, Peanut," I said. "Nobody's going to do anything to me out there."

She gazed at me steadily. She reminded me of Holiness women I'd known in Alabama, with graying, uncut hair and a face etched by years of getting by on not much more than faith and general wariness. Like them, she was probably a prophetess.

"I like you, Mr. Covington," she said. "I don't want anything to happen to you."

And for a long time nothing did. Mr. Read still intended to survey the land. Problem was, the crews he sent out kept getting lost or stuck in the mud, or maybe a little scared themselves. It was a while longer before Mr. Read called with the good news that the corners had been staked. "I figured it'd surprise you," he said. "After two years, you deserve it."

I took the next flight down to Tampa and picked up my old Jeep from a storage place near the airport, but by the time I got to River Ranch, somebody had already pulled up a couple of the wooden survey stakes, torn up my "no trespassing" signs, and driven a swamp buggy over the pitiable dog-wire fence I'd erected around the place.

Back in Birmingham, my friend Bill Murray, an attorney, told me that in order to assert rightful ownership of the land, I might need to do it in what the law termed a "notorious" (or "open" and "noteworthy") fashion. Even a legal survey might not be able to blunt a claim of adverse possession, in the remote case that someone else actually erected a structure and started squatting on my land.

So I decided to build a cabin, a dream I'd had even before Dad died: a primitive retreat with a well, windmill, and kerosene heater, a place where I could write in solitude and where the family could take wilderness vacations. It would be right in the middle of the Hunt Club's self-proclaimed hunting area, and I figured that fact alone would meet the definition of "notorious."

The Good Part

My sister Jeanie has lupus, and occasionally, when her brain swells to the point that she gets confused and starts having seizures, she has to go to the hospital to have her blood cleansed. It's a painful process that Jeanie endures by telling stories. The last time Vicki and I visited her in the hospital, Jeanie was telling us about a pair of shoes her husband, Bunky Wolaver, had found at a discount shoe mart in Birmingham. The shoes were Florsheim Imperial wingtips, an expensive line of men's dress shoes, but this pair was on sale for $5.88. "You know Bunky," Jeanie said. "He couldn't pass up a bargain like that."

The only problem was that the shoes were a size six, and Bunky wears a size nine and a half. So he had been trying for days to find some man who could wear a size-six dress shoe. That morning, for instance, he had phoned Jeanie just as one of her doctors, Dr. Birdley, was making his rounds.

"I'm so glad Dr. Birdley is there," Bunky told her. "How about leaning over the bed and seeing if you can tell what size feet he has."

A few hours later, another lupus patient, a member of Jeanie's support group at the hospital, stopped by to give her encouragement. For the most part, this was a somber visit, as both women are in advanced stages of the disease. But when Jeanie told her friend about Bunky's Florsheim Imperial wingtips, the other lupus patient started laughing so hard, she almost fell out of her chair.

Jeanie's stories have always seemed particularly Southern to me, filled with that wry, dark humor that Southerners seem to revel in, and on the way home from the hospital that night, Vicki and I entered a serious discussion about the nature of Southern storytelling. The good part of Jeanie's story, I thought, was when Bunky asked her to check out the size of her doctor's feet to see if the shoes he had bought on sale might fit. Vicki thought the good part of the story was the moment when the other lupus patient almost fell out of her chair.

We didn't resolve the issue, but we did conclude that every story, Southern or not, has to have a good part. "Have you gotten to the good part yet?" we often ask each other when one of us is reading a novel the other has recommended.

But what exactly constitutes the good part of a story? And since our lives themselves are stories, where in this sea of misery, this vale of tears, does the good part lie?

The answer itself is a story, I think.

When I was a boy, my friend Bert Butts and I decided to sell armadillos. We'd seen an ad in a magazine called *Fur, Fish, and Game.* The ad said that Wild Animal Enterprises of Port Arthur, Texas, was offering a dozen armadillos for $36. Bert and I had never seen an armadillo, but they were only three dollars apiece. If we sold them in Birmingham for, say, $12 each, we'd quadruple our money.

So we sent a money order to Wild Animal Enterprises in the amount of $36 for a dozen armadillos. Then we placed our own ad in our local paper, *The Birmingham News*: "Armadillos, $12," followed by my phone number. The response was overwhelming. "What kind of dog is this ar*mah*-dillo?" one caller asked. Another caller, an apartment dweller, ordered two after we told him they didn't bark. We promised another armadillo to a young married couple just starting out. Within a day or two, we had sold all twelve armadillos.

The only problem was that the armadillos never arrived from Port Arthur, Texas. We tried to call Wild Animal Enterprises, but the place wasn't even listed in directory assistance.

About that time, and quite coincidentally, my father's oldest brother, Uncle Brother, had a heart attack. Uncle Brother was my favorite uncle. He had fought in World War I, and he happened to live in Galveston, Texas. He even had a wife named Texas. Uncle Brother and Aunt Texas.

"Don't you think you ought to go visit Uncle Brother?" I asked my father. Dad had recently lost his job at the steel mill, and he was reading the help-wanted ads.

"Why? Brother's doing fine," Dad said. "He should be out of the hospital in a day or two."

"But he had a heart attack," I said.

"Uh-huh."

"And he lives in Texas."

"Oh," Dad said. He put away his newspaper. "I think I see what you mean. You'd probably like to go to Texas with me, wouldn't you? Maybe on the way to Galveston, we could stop in Port Arthur."

Are you at the good part yet?

The very next day, Dad and Bert and I left for Galveston to visit Uncle Brother. It was a fourteen-hour drive. On the way, we stopped in Port Arthur to look up Wild Animal Enterprises. The company proved to be nothing more than a ramshackle frame house with a couple of caged skunks and a barn owl on the front porch. The man who lived at the address, a Mr. Kenneth Foote, said he'd been trying for weeks to fill our order for armadillos, but the weather had been too dry. The armadillos were all holed up in their burrows somewhere.

"Y'all try again after we get a good rain," he said. Then he returned our money order for $36.

When we arrived in Galveston, Uncle Brother was doing fine. He and Aunt Texas were also very surprised to see us.

"You come all the way from Birmingham?" Aunt Texas asked.

Are you at the good part yet?

After the trip west, Bert and I had to do something, so we ordered our armadillos from another outfit, this one in Florida. The animals were more expensive, though, and we hadn't factored in the shipping costs. In short, it looked as if we were going to lose money on our armadillo venture, but the worst part was that I had not yet gotten to see an armadillo.

When the crates from Florida finally arrived, I was at summer camp. Bert distributed all but two of the armadillos to our customers. He wanted me to be in on delivering the last two. But on the night before I returned from camp, my father, who was keeping the armadillos in a cage in our garage, forgot to secure the latch to the cage. The next morning, when I got home and ran to the garage to see the armadillos, I found the cage empty. The armadillos had escaped.

It was a blow to both me and my father. In retrospect, though, I can see that I was merely disappointed; my father seemed injured in a permanent way. He knew how much I had wanted to see those armadillos, and he felt entirely responsible for their escape. What he didn't understand was that this had been no ordinary summer. I was almost thirteen. When I looked into the empty cage that morning, I had quickly moved past my own disappointment to his. I think this was the first time I had ever allowed someone else's pain to supersede my own. I see this only in retrospect, having been married now for more than twenty years and with children of my own. I hurt for my father because I knew that, in ways, he had invested more in those armadillos than I had. And because he was so much older, time would repay him less generously.

Are you at the good part yet?

My father and I remained close until his death in 1988. He had lived to see the births of our two girls, Ashley and Laura, and his last words to me were about them. "Don't worry about me," he said. "I'll be fine. You just go on home and take care of your family."

There have been other tragedies along the way, including the deaths of my oldest brother and his son, Vicki's parents, and now my mom. But the past fifteen years have been good ones: spend-the-night parties and softball games and pets too numerable to mention by species, let alone name.

But two springs ago, things took a bad turn. And that July, Vicki and I had a fight, an all-day, frantic, shoot-em-up. It was fueled by jealousy, and it was low and vicious, like nothing we'd ever experienced before. We said unspeakable things that made no sense outside the pathology of our particular marriage. Until that quarrel, I'd never even thought of our marriage as having a pathology.

And then July came along.

Are you at the good part yet?

Two days after the fight, Laura and I flew to central Florida for a long-anticipated camping trip, just the two of us, something my father and I had never done, unless you count that trip to Texas with my friend Bert to visit Uncle Brother in Galveston.

Laura and I pitched our tent at Lake Kissimmee State Park, a few miles from the patch of palmetto scrubland Dad had bought more than thirty years before. I told Laura all about Dad deeding the land to me before he died, and about the Hunt Club. I told her I was determined to reclaim my inheritance, no matter how insignificant it might appear to be.

As Laura and I drove past a fire tower near the intersection of Highways 60 and 630, I pointed out the window and said, "Straight through those trees lies the property your granddaddy left us."

At precisely that moment, we saw an armadillo on the side of the road. I pulled onto the shoulder, and we walked back to the spot where the armadillo was rooting around in the grass. A few feet away lay another armadillo, crushed by a passing car.

I picked up the surviving armadillo. He was young, a juvenile. He didn't appear to be injured. He waved his sturdy legs at me and blinked his eyes.

"Can we keep him?" Laura asked.

I took the armadillo as a sign. "You better believe we're going to keep him," I told her.

Are you at the good part yet?

We put the armadillo into an empty Styrofoam ice chest until we could get to a hardware store in Frostproof and buy a wire rabbit hutch. We assembled the hutch right there in the store; the salesman helped. And then we took the armadillo to the local cafe for breakfast. Nobody there had ever seen a live one that close up before.

Next, we took the armadillo to the front gate of the Hunt Club. The animal was a conversation piece. Sandy Edwards, the wife of the Hunt Club's president, said she had some articles about armadillos that I might be interested in. If I gave her my name and address, she said she'd send the articles to me, so of course I did. Then Thelma McQueen raised the gate and let us in. The land was a wilderness of palmetto and pine, lily pads and frog song, Laura's idea of paradise. I was glad she'd been able to see it at last, and I resolved anew to get our part of it back.

But there were complications in this armadillo story of ours. When we left River Ranch, the ranger at the state park where we'd camped wouldn't let us bring the armadillo in, so we had to find a vet who would board him for the night. It took a little persuasion. But that night we slept soundly for the first time during our camping trip.

The next morning, we stopped by the vet's office and picked up the armadillo. We bought a pet carrier designed to fit under an airplane seat, and the vet gave us documents so we could take the armadillo with us on the flight from Tampa to Birmingham.

"Does this mean we can really keep him?" Laura asked.

I nodded.

"Then I think we should call him Joey," she said. Joey was the name of the girls' Sunday School teacher, a longtime family friend.

But in Tampa we discovered our airline didn't allow animals on board, not even in the cargo bins. Another airline did allow animals, at an exorbitant price, but there was one stipulation. "They have to be warm-blooded," the clerk said.

"But he is warm-blooded," Laura said. "He's a mammal."

"Well, all I know is he's not a dog or cat," the clerk replied. "We can't fly an armadillo to Birmingham."

So Laura and I didn't fly to Birmingham, either. We rented a car instead. It took us two days, but we had our armadillo.

Are you at the good part yet?

That Sunday afternoon, tired and proud, we brought Joey into the kitchen of our house in Birmingham and set him on the table for Vicki and Ashley to admire. Joey was asleep, so we didn't take him out of the cage.

"Is he all right?" Laura asked.

"Sure," I said. "He's fine."

But later, Joey started breathing through his mouth and wheezing, exactly as my father had done toward the end of his life. I tried not to panic. I left a message on our vet's answering machine. "I know you don't usually treat armadillos," I said, "but we have one here who appears to have a cold."

By the time our vet returned the call, Joey was dead.

Wait a minute. What happened to the good part?

I don't think the good part of a story is the same as the turning point, or critical moment, or "denouement," whatever that is. I think the good part comes much earlier than that. I think the good part is the moment things get really interesting, when a story that is meandering aimlessly along suddenly seems to know in which direction to head. I don't mean the point where complications arise, because I think the good part of a story has more to do with character than with incident. The good part demands a surrender from the reader. You relinquish a little piece of your life and fall heedlessly into the lives of the story's characters. If they head for Texas, by golly you're going, too. If they get armadillos on the brain, well, so do you. The good part of the story is the indispensable part. It is the part where you know you won't be able to put the story down.

But what about our lives? The good part, for me, has been elusive.

That fight Vicki and I had in July was not all that unusual for a couple to have, married as long as we'd been.

But I had never been more aware of how precarious our marriage was. We were hanging by a slender thread. And when a July like that one comes along, I wish I could check into the hospital, as Jeanie must do, and have my blood completely cleansed.

Like her, I think I could bear the pain by telling stories—stories with good parts in them. I know there must have been a good part to our story that July. On its precise beginning, though, Vicki and I will disagree. I think the good part of the story may have begun the moment Laura and I passed the piece of property my father had left us, and we saw the armadillo rooting in the grass along the shoulder of the road. Or maybe it was the moment I picked him up, and Laura said, "Can we keep him?" and I knew in a flash that we would try.

But Vicki thinks the good part of the story came later, on the day after Joey died, when she came into the kitchen and found Laura crying.

"Are you crying about Joey?" Vicki asked.

Laura shook her head. "I'm crying for Dad."

We buried Joey in our side yard, where we had buried our favorite golden retriever and innumerable frogs, chipmunks, and mice. Then we tried to replace him with a green iguana the girls named Javy, after Javy Lopez, the catcher for the Atlanta Braves. Ashley lets Javy climb up the front of her shirt, but Laura has had trouble warming to him. Tonight, though, as I write this, she is feeding him a strawberry by hand.

And I am thinking about armadillos past and present. Who could have foreseen that an armadillo would come again into the life of my family, that it would leave us as suddenly as the others had, and that Laura would bear my pain in the same way I had borne my father's?

The Canvas House

I chose a design from a book called *Tiny Houses*, by Lester Walker. Although the cabin consisted of a wooden frame and a deck floor, its walls were made of canvas, with intricately sewn zippered windows and doors. The structure had been designed by architect James Hadley for permanent use at a resort on the island of St. John in the U.S. Virgin Islands. One of a series of well-ventilated cottages, linked by raised walkways, it made for an attractive and ecologically friendly getaway.

Hadley's design had two important advantages in addition to aesthetic beauty. The cabin would be permanent enough to make the desired statement about my ownership of the land—open and notorious—but temporary enough, especially if I bolted the frame together and stapled the canvas sides, so that Polk County authorities might look the other way in regard to building and sanitation codes.

I don't know why I worried about this so much. The county had never enforced building or sanitation codes against Hunt Club members who had erected hundreds of structures on *other* people's land. When I asked sheriff's deputy Gene Smith why not, he said the answer was simple: "If we were going to cite anybody for violations, it would have to be the people who owned the land." Then again, it might have had something to do with the fact that the director of the Polk County building department was himself a member of the Hunt Club.

The element of surprise being essential, I figured I'd have to assemble the structure in Birmingham, break it apart, and truck it down to central Florida myself. The fabrication of the walls, windows, and doors would be the most difficult part of the construction process. I went to a number of companies, but the owners, who seemed to specialize in commercial awnings and outdoor weddings, just didn't understand what it was I wanted or why.

I finally found a small outfit in Pell City, Alabama, that was willing to take on the task, as soon as they finished some tents they'd promised for the 1996 Atlanta Olympic Games. Bob Clayton, the owner of the company, immediately grasped the intentions of the project. He, too, believed in claiming your inheritance, no matter how worthless it might appear to be. He was a generous man and quoted a fair price. I would like to think Bob had literary insight as well, but perhaps he was merely curious about what the Hunt Club might do to me in the end.

Bob's seamstress, Jane Mitchell, accomplished the grueling work with skill and cheerfulness. She did add a cautionary note after she'd double-sewn the last seam and installed the last zippered window, with its elaborate Velcro snaps: "If you ever need any more of these, please don't come back to me."

I had thought the framing of the cabin would be easy. But I'd never even framed a recipe box. Fact is, I squeaked through manual training with a D back in the eighth grade, and although my father, who had taken up carpentry as an antidote to depression, worked patiently with me in my formative years, at midlife I was still unversed in the subtleties of driving a nail.

That's where friends Jim Neel and Wayne Cook came in. We hammered and bolted the thing together in my front yard ("Whatcha doing, Mister Dennis?" a neighborhood boy asked). Then we broke down the frame and loaded it and the canvas walls into a Toyota four-by-four pickup that I'd bought from a friend whose lover had left her. The only improvement I made to the truck was to scrape off the Tasmanian Devil decal. Then it was Florida or bust.

I drove all night and met Jim's plane at the Tampa airport. He drove the Jeep; I drove the truck. And we set out for River Ranch. The start of the general gun season was still a couple of days off, but musket and archery were finishing up, so there was ample hubbub around the front gate for Jim and me to get through without arousing anybody's suspicion about the material weighing down the truckbed.

Only after we had reached the property, unloaded the truck, erected the corner posts, and hung the floor joists did people begin to take note.

"What the fuck you think you're doing?" shouted one hunter from the buckboard of a speeding swamp buggy.

"What's it look like?" Jim shouted back, but I don't think the hunter heard him. Jim had once been a hunter himself, a duck hunter, and he was therefore inclined toward a certain civility that precluded trespassing on other people's property or shouting "fuck" from the top of a swamp buggy.

As the canvas walls went up, a trio of bow hunters in camouflage stopped by to see what we were up to. These hunters were from the Atlantic Coast, around Vero Beach, and they had been patiently stalking deer all morning. They didn't come onto the property until I invited them, and they had nothing but praise for the design of the cabin. We parted with mutual wishes of good luck.

They were definitely in the minority, though. "Stupid sons of bitches!" other hunters would shout. "Assholes! Shitheads! Don't you know you can't do that?"

Every ratty old pickup or swamp buggy seemed to bring another load of angry hunters shouting epithets.

"What's *your* names?" I would shout back at them. But the hunters simply glared at me as their swamp buggies lurched on, exhaling a foul miasma of exhaust.

In the heat of the early afternoon, Jim and I took a break, just when the official delegation from the Hunt

Club arrived. There were three men, armed with high-powered rifles despite the fact that the general gun season hadn't started yet, and they drove their buggy right up to the unfinished cabin.

"According to the laws of the Hunt Club, you can't do this," announced one of the men. He identified himself as the delegate in charge of the Northeast Division, whatever the hell that was.

"Can't do what?" I asked.

"Put up a camp here."

I asked him if he had a camp.

"Sure."

"Whose land is your camp on?" I asked.

The delegate glanced at the other two. "I have no idea."

"Well, I know whose land my camp is on," I said.

"Whose?" he asked.

"Mine."

The delegate seemed struck by that. "He's had it surveyed," one of the other guys whispered to him, and a thought appeared to flicker behind the delegate's eyes.

"I've got land, too," he said. "Course, I don't know where it is. It might be up near Kicco," he added.

"Probably under water," the third man said.

For some reason, this fact seemed to suggest a commonality of interest among us. The men relaxed their grips on their rifles and looked around, as though seeing the place for the first time. "All this used to be owned by the Gulf American Corporation," the delegate explained. "This is one of the original Florida land scandals."

I told him my father had clear title to the land and had left it to me before he died.

The delegate's eyes narrowed. His jaw hardened. He'd apparently heard something about this kind of thing before. "Do you have a notarized transfer of deed signed by witnesses?"

I nodded.

"And you recorded it in the courthouse in Bartow?"

I nodded again.

"It's his land," one of the other men reminded him.

"Hmm," the delegate said. "Well, just so long as you know the rules. You can't put up a camp in the hunting area, only in the camping area."

I repeated that I was putting up the camp on my own land.

The delegate pondered that fact for the longest time, and then he changed the subject to the insolence of teenagers in this day and age. "Not like it used to be in the olden times," he said. And that's how we left it, a Mexican standoff.

When Jim and I finished the cabin, it was long past dark. We'd considered sleeping in the cabin that night, but I told Jim this wasn't his fight. We'd sleep at a motel in Bartow, and I'd make sure he caught his flight back to Birmingham the next morning.

As we passed the Mirees' camp on the way out, one of the hunters around an open bonfire said, "There goes that son of a bitch."

Still, I hadn't anticipated the terror I'd feel the next night, sitting alone in the canvas house, while on the ridge above me, a thousand hunters gathered to wait for dawn and the start of the general gun season. Campfires flickered through the trees, and there was an occasional burst of practice rounds, followed by whoops of triumph or derision. I imagined I was on some Civil War battleground, Antietam the night before the sunken road, the cornfield, the piles of corpses, the defeat.

Most of that night I sat cross-legged on the bunk with a machete in my lap, waiting for the enemy charge, but at some point I fell into a deep, mind-numbing sleep, waking only once as the endless procession of swamp buggies rumbled by my cabin before dawn. I fell asleep again and didn't wake until full light.

"There's always one asshole in the bunch!" someone shouted from a swamp buggy. "Goddamn dickhead!"

"He ain't been shot yet?" another one asked.

I was puttering outside the cabin, warming up Beenie-Weenies on my camp stove and occasionally catching the chatter on my CB radio. I wore an orange deer hunter's cap and had tied an orange flag to the antenna of the Jeep. One of the six-foot four-by-four posts on the cabin deck was even painted orange from top to bottom. If they wanted to shoot me, they couldn't claim they didn't know I was there.

That afternoon, I sat at the writing desk I'd made and took some notes. When the light began to fail, I turned on my Coleman battery-operated lantern. All day, there had been shots nearby, but I hadn't worried much about them until I heard some that sounded much too close for comfort. I stepped outside to see where these new shots were coming from. About twenty yards from the cabin, beneath a circle of pines where two buggy trails intersected, a handful of men were drinking beer and shooting into the palmetto, apparently at nothing in particular. They looked like the kind of men that hung around the Mirees' campfire, hog hunters in half-soled rubber boots and grimy work caps. They were chewing tobacco, and the laughter after they spit had something familiar to it, a sharp, malicious edge. They were like my people back in Alabama, and maybe that's what scared me the most.

I waited until they finally moved farther down the road. Then I took my time cleaning up the place so they wouldn't sense my urgency if they happened to be watching secretly from the palmetto brakes. I zipped up the door of the cabin but otherwise left it as it was, the Coleman lantern burning at my writing desk. Then I cranked up the Jeep and drove to the nearest motel, the Indian Lake, to spend the night. I'd probably been a fool to spend the night before the opening of hunting season in a canvas cabin with a machete in my lap. I wasn't going to be twice a fool by staying there over a Saturday night.

The next morning I drove through the front gate while it was still dark and reached the cabin just as the sun was lightening the eastern sky. There were two bullet holes to the left of the cabin door. One of the bullets had blasted the Coleman lantern to pieces. The far wall was filled with exit holes from all the debris. The other bullet, had I been sitting in my customary place at the writing desk, would have gone right through my chest.

Peanut was behind the counter when I signed out at the front gate. I told her what had happened, and she shook her head sadly. "You do have dishonest people out here. I lost seventy-two bags of ice in the month of November. But I can't believe somebody would shoot up your camp."

"Maybe it was just some kids," I offered.

"Or drunks," she said. "We've got quite a lot of them around. At least I've got a CB handle for you now."

"What?"

"Buckshot," she said.

The sheriff's deputy sent to write up the crime report met me in the parking lot of the Kissimmee River Restaurant. He was clean-cut and professional-looking, but he didn't go out to the property itself, and he didn't offer much hope. "If you'd been in the cabin at the time of the shooting, it'd be a different matter. As it is, the charge is just a misdemeanor, firing into an unoccupied dwelling. It's not worth investigating any further unless something else were to happen. I hope nothing does. In the meantime, we all know what this is about. Those bullets didn't get there by accident. They were meant to intimidate you."

His words sealed my resolve. The land per se was no longer the issue. What would drive me now was my full recognition of the principle involved. My father believed in justice, and although he might not have agreed on my methods, he certainly would have understood the motivation behind them. I would not be cowed by threats of violence. I wanted justice, and I wanted it now.

So I did what I figured any self-respecting Alabama boy would have done. I raided my piggy bank to purchase two parcels of land on either side of mine for $1,800 in back taxes, just so the Hunt Club would know they hadn't scared me off. And then I bought a gun.

I'd never owned a gun before. I'd been scared of them ever since my childhood friend Eugene Beaman shot himself in the head while playing Russian roulette with a revolver he'd found in his father's underwear drawer. Other neighborhood kids were present and playing the game with him. I'm glad I wasn't. I got to the Beamans' house in time to see the attendants carry Eugene's body to the ambulance under a heavy white sheet. His funeral was the first I ever attended. I thought Eugene would be at the very bottom of the casket, so I put my head in so far our noses touched. It's a sensation I never want to experience again.

This gun I bought was a Rossi .357 magnum, and I even started to relish using it for target practice just as the swamp buggies carrying men who'd called me "dickhead" passed by. They didn't shout insults anymore, but

they did start leaving presents for me in my absence—
the guts from a hog carcass strung across my fence or a
box of human shit on the doorstep of my cabin, just
something for me to remember them by.

One weekend my former Baptist preacher, Dale
Chambliss, came down to visit. He brought his shotgun,
and I'd borrowed another one that had belonged to
Vicki's grandfather. Between those two shotguns and the
revolver, I figured we were well covered at close range,
but of course the hunters had rifles with long-range
scopes, so it wasn't likely to be an entirely easy few
days.

"Why don't we just draw targets on our backs?" Dale
suggested.

When I introduced him to Peanut, she had another
suggestion: "You're his preacher. Why don't you talk
him into putting his cabin in the camping area?"

Dale just laughed.

"I mean it," Peanut said. "He's got his cabin in the
hunting area, and his property's right there on the line.
Come back in the camping area, and he'll be fine."

"He's got a mind of his own," Dale said.

"I know, but sometimes you got to bend your mind a
little bit and back up."

Peanut's daughter was itching to show Dale the five-
foot diamondback rattlesnake she'd shot with a .22. She
said the snake was in the freezer.

But Peanut hadn't finished yet. "Why don't you do
that?" she said to me. "And then you won't get shot at,
you know. And I won't have to feel like I'm responsible."

I told her it wasn't her responsibility.

"Yes, it is," she said. "You don't have to camp on your own property. It's the honor system here. Everybody knows they're camping on somebody else's property."

I told her I didn't want to camp on somebody else's land.

Peanut's daughter, a barefoot teen with waist-length hair, finally talked us into taking the discussion out to the freezer, where she'd laid the snake out on a bed of ice. Its eyes were fixed under a patina of frost.

"Pretty good shot, isn't she?" Peanut said, and she gave her daughter a hug.

I'd grown fond of the canvas house. After I patched the bullet and debris holes, it was a great place to spend the week, mosquito-proof and well-ventilated. After the fall quarter ended at the university, I went to River Ranch every chance I had. During the day I'd work outside, driving fence posts or clearing brush from around the corner stakes. During breaks, I'd take target practice at empty Beenie-Weenie cans. At night, I'd write a little while, or read, and then I'd fall dead asleep. Dawn was always the best, cool and quiet except for the birds.

I rarely heard a gunshot during the week. Weekends were another matter. I didn't stay in the canvas house on weekends. Too many hunters. Too much drinking. Too many guns.

If Dale hadn't visited, I probably wouldn't have stayed that weekend. But he wouldn't have it any other way.

He was crazy like that, a Huntsville preacher's son with a lifelong addiction to danger. When he was a teenager, he and some friends got hold of some dynamite. The sheriff's department found it in a caddie shack on the country club golf course. They said it was enough to blow a couple of Huntsville blocks off the map.

Dale had always made me a little nervous on this account, but I was grateful he had felt the urge to bring a shotgun with him to help defend my property. I needed a warm body to hide behind, even if it belonged to the preacher who had baptized me—even better, for that reason, that he take the first round.

We had fun strutting around the property with our weapons in hand. It was like being nineteen again, in love with all things male. We shot at targets and hammered nails and pretended to investigate the crime scene, using string to plot the trajectory of the bullets that had been fired through the canvas walls. "That wasn't an accident," we concluded, as though the issue had ever been in doubt.

Then we hand-drilled a shallow well. We even saw a space shuttle launch way off in the distance, a spectacular and unexpected sight. It was just like the TV commentators say; it rose on a column of fire. Otherwise, the weekend went without incident.

Dale seemed disappointed. I guess he had been counting on some kind of flesh wound, at least. And I was surprised myself that the hunters hadn't threatened us again, or even shouted insults. I hoped Dale didn't think

I'd exaggerated the situation just to sharpen the sense of adventure for us both.

But it didn't surprise me, when I next went to River Ranch alone, to discover that the Hunt Club had hit me again, this time smashing the windshield and the rear windows of the Jeep, ripping the walls of the cabin with knives, and stealing just about everything from both, including my cots, chairs, writing desk, and a solar panel I had used to keep my Jeep battery charged. In the center of the cabin floor, they'd left another calling card, a dead armadillo lying on its back.

L ater that day, I happened to see Pete Edwards standing just inside the front gate. He was dressed fit to kill in his pressed jeans, plaid shirt, western boots, and Stetson, and he looked to be having a good time greeting hunters as they came through the gate. They'd shout encouragement to him and he'd duck and grin or take his Stetson off and make a little bow as though he were running for public office. Fact is, he had just dethroned Alan Ingram, in a brief and bloodless coup, after Ingram reminded the members, by means of a Hunt Club newsletter, that they owned only a fraction of the land at River Ranch and so might have a difficult time as Dick Powell's legal challenges moved through the courts.

"Mr. Pete," I said, "you're just the man I wanted to see." He smiled and shook my hand as though he hadn't yet made my acquaintance.

"By the way, what happened to Alan?" I asked. "I thought he was president now."

"Wife problems," Pete said.

I nodded sympathetically, and then I told him my camp had been shot up a second time.

Pete's smile didn't waver. "There've been about forty camps broke into this year, for food and whiskey and other things," he said. "But I don't know why they'd tear your camp all to hell."

I told him I thought he did know why.

"Well, the rules are you can't camp in the hunting area."

I asked him who had drawn the line between the camping area and the hunting area.

He took off his Stetson and literally scratched behind his ear. "The cow man?" he said. And then apparently hearing the lack of conviction in his own voice, he added: "Okay, whoever. I don't know who drew the line."

I told him I'd been threatened by members of the club before the shootings.

"I don't know anybody in here who'd be that damn stupid," he said, and by now his smile had clearly begun to fade. "These men just go in, pick a spot, and clear it for their camp. They know it ain't their property. They have no intentions of doing harm to anybody's property."

He shouted another greeting to a hog hunter with a truckload of pit bulls. "Sure, they take offense when somebody like you comes in," he whispered. "They think, 'He wants to steal my property.'"

I reminded him that the cabin and Jeep were on my property to begin with.

"I own land back here, too," he said, not smiling now. "And in order to protect my property, I have to protect everybody else's."

I told him I didn't know where he'd gotten a crazy idea like that, but if he really believed it was his duty to protect my land, he'd done a pretty lousy job of it.

"I want you to come out and see my camp," I said.

"I've done seen it," Pete answered, and he put his Stetson back on with a settling twist that allowed me to understand the conversation was over.

The sheriff's deputy who filed the crime report about the second incident was red-faced and barrel-chested, a former member of the Hunt Club who'd become irked by the illogic of it all.

"It's the same damn thing that's been going on out here for thirty-something years," he said.

With a flourish of his ballpoint pen, this deputy added two felonies to the report: burglary and grand theft. There were no official suspects as yet in either of the shooting incidents, he said, although the first deputy had told me the Mirees were very familiar faces down at headquarters, and this deputy said he figured it probably was them.

"They're out there poaching," he said. "Are they still living in that school bus?"

I told him yes.

"They're just lowlife scum bums," he said. "They ought to be shot. That's the problem these days. You've got these scum bums that you can't kill."

He said that at least the Miree boys knew how to wear their underwear right.

I made the mistake of asking how.

"Yellow to the front and brown to the back." He laughed a thick, phlegm-coated laugh.

"Country's just gone to hell," he said. "We're trying to govern a country in the year 2000 with a Constitution that gave all these people these fucking rights."

I mentioned that my land was surveyed.

"So you're the one," he said.

"How'd you know that?"

"Oh, I just heard there was a guy out there who'd had his land surveyed."

I asked if he was going to take a look at the cabin.

"No, we're not going out there today," he said. "Of course, if somebody gets killed, we'll have to."

The Camouflage Man

After this second attack, I retired to the Polk County courthouse and tax assessor's office in Bartow, where I pored over the plat maps of River Ranch Acres. I was in a fever to find another way onto Dad's property, a way that would avoid the Hunt Club's gate entirely. Membership in the club had gained me what I'd needed—access to the land while I waited for it to be surveyed, and a window of opportunity during which Jim and I could erect the canvas house. But from that moment on, my cover was blown. As Dick Powell told me in a late-night phone conversation, I was a "double agent" now. He expected reprisals once they discovered he and I were in cahoots. "They're gonna kill you," he said at the time. "I'm numero uno on their list. You're numero dos."

Powell's personal war with Pete Edwards had meanwhile reached a critical point. After fifteen years of acrimonious litigation, it had all come down to this: whether one man had the right to access his land along a deeded easement. Were Powell's deed and the easements referred to in it worth the paper they were recorded on, or not? And how would a judge's decision affect the rest of us, the thousands of other landowners who had been shut out by the Hunt Club? The future of River Ranch hung in the balance, and both sides seemed ready in case events took another bad turn.

Dick Powell had obtained a permit to carry a concealed weapon. Otherwise, he sounded optimistic. "The Hunt Club is going to go ape-shit," he said. "As simple as this suit is, it's the crux. They can be mean and violent and spit on you, but when they lose the ability to fence the access points, they're finished."

I'd come too far on my own, and lost too much already, to wait while the wheels of justice ground on. I had claimed my property in a notorious fashion, and now I needed to be able to protect what was left of it. Powell's suit concerned his access, not mine. I needed a section line of my own in order to claim an access point, and after an afternoon of searching the records, I found what I was looking for. It had been there in plain sight.

Even if the sheriff's department refused to recognize the legitimacy of access along the borders of individual tracts, I didn't see how they could continue indefinitely to disallow access to the interior of River Ranch by public rights-of-way along section lines. Dad's two and a half acres did not touch a section line. But one of the parcels I had bought for back taxes after the first shooting incident did. Surely, I must have known that at the time. Maybe I hadn't understood the issues well enough to make the connection. But in the hothouse of the tax assessor's office, I did. And the beautiful thing about it, the symmetrical and grace-filled detail, was that the parcel of land where the section line intersected Highway 60—the parcel containing the access point—was owned by Franklin Tolliver, the squinty-eyed old bastard who'd lost his fortune in the bordello business and who, although he hadn't allowed me to use his back gate (because of prior agreement with the Hunt Club), could hardly deny me the right to walk his property line. Like me, he was an Alabama boy!

I slammed the plat book shut and gave Tolliver a call at his home in Haines City. No one answered the phone, so I drove out to his place on Highway 60 in hope of catching him there. No one was at home. But in the process, I made a second startling discovery. The five-acre parcel adjoining Tolliver's along that section line was for sale. I didn't have any money for such a purchase, but it was the idea that counted. There were two ways to secure an access point to my land at River Ranch, and the enormity of my good luck floored me. If Tolliver refused to let me walk his property line, I could still buy the parcel next to his and walk my own!

The next morning I was parked in front of Tolliver's front gate when he pulled in. I told him I'd come to see if he had piglets yet; I wanted to ease into this discussion about the section line, and he seemed happy enough to see me, so I thought so far, so good. After he unlocked the gate, the breeze lifted a curl of his sparse white hair. "Two of them piglets died," he said, screwing up his good eye. "But the others are fine, if the hawk don't get them. I killed a rattlesnake last week right here at the gate. Watch your step coming around the truck."

The piglets were precious, as far as piglets go. To sustain my enthusiasm for them, I had to talk about what Ashley and Laura might think.

"Those are pretty names," Tolliver said. "For girls."

I waited for the punchline.

"I had boys," he finally said. "Two of them. Well, one's a stepson, but he's closer to me than the other one. We own this place together. He's a Franklin, too, but sometimes we call him Phil. His last name's different, of course."

I figured it was safe to get down to business. "How much you reckon they're asking for that piece?" I nodded toward the parcel for sale.

Tolliver didn't even look up. "I done bought that. Signed the papers last night."

I felt my heart drop.

"It was five acres," he said, "and I don't mind telling you the price was dear. But we've got to have something to protect us from all the development they got planned. Somebody's coming in with a gun shop. There'll be a fucking hamburger stand before long."

I explained why I had been interested in the parcel, reminded him of the land Dad had left me, the access problem created by the Hunt Club. That's why I'd asked about a key to his back gate. I wasn't trying to pull one on him.

"We've got this agreement with the Hunt Club."

"I understand," I said. "But here's the thing."

"Wait a minute. My boy will probably want to hear this."

I turned to see a man in a white T-shirt descend the trailer steps. He appeared to be in his early thirties, lean and fit, with a full head of hair sculpted into a ducktail in back. The whiteness of his shirt was emphasized by the darkness of the man's arms, which were evenly tanned and burnished red underneath. This was a man who worked shirtless outside, and I knew in an instant that if he'd been shirtless at that moment, I'd have seen a tattoo on his right deltoid: F. J., Franklin Jackson. I remembered him from the Hunt Club gatehouse, on a day when two fat boys, nephews of his, had been weighing a hog they insisted they'd killed by mistake. I could almost remember the sound of the boys' voices, the flat, matter-of-fact twang.

"This is the one I was talking about, my stepson. He's a Franklin, too, but it's not because we're blood kin. Just call him anything."

I wondered, as I shook his hand, if he remembered me from that day, but I decided from the way his eyes skidded away that he didn't, or if he did, didn't want to acknowledge it. After all, we hadn't spoken a word at the time. It was just the boys' story about the hog, and what Franklin Jackson wrote in the Hunt Club notebook: *the fat boys* instead of a name.

"I was telling this man here from Alabama about our back gate," Franklin said.

"We've got an agreement," his stepson said.

I told him I knew that, but I was wondering if something else couldn't be worked out. I owned some land back in what used to be called River Ranch Acres, my dad had left it to me and so on, and there was a public right-of-way to it along the section line here.

"Who told you that?" the stepson said. There was nothing in his voice to suggest anything but a detached curiosity.

"Every section line is like that," I said, more to Franklin Tolliver than to him. I didn't want to risk a complication with my plan.

"I don't have a problem with somebody walking the fence line," Tolliver said, "as long as I know beforehand. Otherwise, I'll shoot that sucker dead."

I smiled as though it had been a joke, which I don't think it was.

"I got a problem with it," the stepson said in the same flat voice that betrayed nothing more than the facts.

I felt trouble coming on. "I'm not down here very often. I just a need a way to check on my land," I explained.

For the first time, the stepson looked at me directly. "That's what everybody who comes around here says."

"Them's mostly hunters, just boys," Franklin said. "My boy doesn't have any kids yet. I tell him he ought to find a woman first." And he made like he needed to do something with his hands, chop wood or feed the cows. Maybe *woman* was a shape he wanted to draw in the air. Instead, he took a pinch of snuff from his watch pocket and tucked it behind his lower lip. It made him sneeze. The dog barked twice, and Franklin Tolliver sneezed again.

"Bless you," his stepson said.

"I promise I won't abuse the privilege," I said.

The stepson turned as if to go.

"It don't matter to me," Tolliver said.

"It's a matter of safety for me and my family. They've shot up my camp, broken the windows in my Jeep."

"That's somebody not from around here," the stepson said.

"I'm not so sure of that," I replied.

"You're not from around here either," he said.

"Shit." Tolliver had stepped in fresh cow manure and momentarily lost his balance. His stepson rushed to steady him, and then let him slide down the length of his body to a sitting position on an overturned bucket.

"It's my land," I said.

"So?" The stepson was starting to get angry now. So was I. This was a clear-cut issue about fundamental property rights, and although the stepson supported those rights in theory, he didn't see any point in letting outsiders call the shots.

"My daddy's not real clear-headed, if you know what I mean," he said. "I'd rather you go through me. And I say no."

I asked him how firm that "no" was.

"I'll not let you or anybody else onto this property without a judge's order in hand, and even then, I might not do it. Judges, especially federal, are the lowest forms of life."

I wasn't getting anywhere with him. I tried again with the elder Franklin, tried to get him thinking and talking about Alabama. Bear Bryant. George Wallace. That kind of thing.

"Why are you carrying on about them?" he asked.

"Hey, I told you to leave my dad alone," the stepson said, and I could see there was no use going any further with this. I'd come up against the final obstacle to an enlightened South—misplaced family loyalty, a love affair with the grave.

Fifty dollars a year, and Franklin Tolliver, his stepson, and their guests had the use of more than 40,000 acres of private land, a substantial wilderness area unregulated, for all practical purposes, by the federal government; subject to only the most general of state hunting laws; exempt from county building and sanitation codes; and protected, by virtue of shared interests, from the meddling of sheriff's deputies, prosecutors, judges, clerks, and other agents of the civil bureaucracy.

Franklin Tolliver didn't even have to walk onto the land to hunt it. He could ride in on a twelve-foot-high swamp buggy, like an Indian rajah atop a jeweled elephant, and the entire landscape of prairie and plains would unroll before him, its creatures to be used or taken as he pleased. All this, for the price of an annual club membership. For the first time, I saw it through their eyes, and understood the way in which we were ultimately alike: The hunters were dreamers, too.

One moonless night, I dressed in black—black jeans, black T-shirt, black windbreaker. I extinguished a candle flame between my thumb and forefinger and smudged the residue under my eyes. For good luck, I put on my black Cafe Loup cap and my belt with the portrait of Jesus on the front. Then I slipped out of my room at the Indian Lake Motel and ducked into the breezeway that led to the lot in back, where I had parked my truck next to a Dempsey Dumpster redolent of cabbage, used diapers, and sesame seed oil.

"You night fishing?" a voice asked.

I turned to see a broad-faced young man in a Florida State baseball cap studded with metallic fish lures.

I shook my head. "You?"

From the way the man's face drained, I figured he must have noticed that I was carrying a shotgun and had a revolver strapped to my chest. The candle black under my eyes didn't help much, either.

"I'm just here for the bass rodeo tomorrow morning," he said in a very small voice.

"Me, too," I said. "Good luck."

The lures on his cap rattled as he nodded and said, "Same to you, mister. Good luck to you."

I started the truck and pulled onto Highway 60 with only my parking lights on. The air that whipped in was fragrant with the smell of burnt oranges from the Citrus

World plant in Lake Wales. About a half mile from Franklin Tolliver's place, I cut the engine and coasted with the clutch engaged into an abandoned stumping road that petered out at the cow man's fence. The stumps had served a host of purposes for the cow hunters who had settled here—fence posts, turpentine, and sawdust for the dynamite plant. Getting out of the truck, I cinched on my black backpack and Boy Scout canteen, then went through my mental checklist: bug spray, compass, GPS, wire cutters, flashlight with red Saran Wrap taped over the bulb. I retrieved the shotgun from the backseat, patted the holstered revolver, and, under cover of stunted magnolias and pine, followed the cow man's fence west until it intersected Franklin Tolliver's property line. There I waited, crouched in the palmetto, until Tolliver's blue-eyed Sheltie stopped barking. He was chained to a chinaberry tree by the hog pen. When I was satisfied that no one was in the trailer to be disturbed if he started up again, I cut the strands of barbed wire and turned each back, paused to familiarize myself with the night sounds, and then stood and entered Franklin Tolliver's property, the ends of the barbed wire catching and then releasing my windbreaker.

The dog still didn't bark. Maybe he recognized my scent. He lay panting with his head thrown back over his shoulder. He was watching me negotiate the railroad ties at the edge of the catfish pond. He must have been watching as I sprinted toward the back fence, cut the strands of barbed wire there, peeled them back, and headed into the muck of River Ranch Acres. That must have been why he finally let out that long, dismal wail, as if I was a culprit just now coming in, instead of going out.

I had pictured myself making a beeline south along the section line until I saw the canvas house. But even with the Saran-wrapped flashlight, I couldn't read my compass or GPS clearly enough. Besides, I'd learned that palmetto and hardwood hammocks were practically impossible to traverse even in broad daylight. So I wound my way back to the nearest buggy trail and gingerly followed it instead. I was scared: scared that a hunter illegally spotlighting deer would catch a glimpse of movement and blow my head off; scared I'd step on a snake; but mostly I was scared because of the radio report I'd heard that afternoon: an African lion had escaped a traveling circus near Kissimmee and was headed in my direction. Sure enough, I came upon a hulking figure in the middle of the trail. It had large, luminous eyes. I almost blew my foot off trying to disengage the shotgun's safety before I realized the silhouette and eyes were those of a cow.

But I was not afraid of the Hunt Club, or at least that's what I was telling myself. I wanted to see some of those characters out after dark. I had this vision of reaching the canvas house right as they were kicking back another round of beers and taking potshots through the zippered windows that Jane Mitchell, that saint from Pell City, Alabama, had so meticulously sewn. I saw my purpose clearly now. This would be a low-intensity but sharp and protracted conflict. The *casus belli* was self-evident, defense of property being the right of all men. Don't tread on me was my humble creed. I was an American by birth and an Alabamian by the grace of God, and I wasn't about to be outmaneuvered or outgunned by a bunch of no-neck Floridians.

But when I finally found the canvas house, it looked forlorn and empty in the vast dark of the peninsular night. I knew, of course, that it was too late to save the cabin and Jeep. I just wanted to prevent further desecration of them. So I poked the barrel of the shotgun into clumps of dried palmetto fans, vaguely hoping that one of the Mirees would offer himself up to be shot. Instead of Mirees, I got mosquitoes and a bad case of the runs. But afterward, I settled into a watchful pose behind one of the downwind pines, and shortly after that, I began to doze.

Gray light woke me. It was dawn. My throat was raw. I had a raging headache. But I figured I had shown the Hunt Club a thing or two. I was so full of myself, I decided to walk away from my cabin and out of River Ranch Acres by way of the Hunt Club gate. I didn't care how ridiculous I looked, or what the leadership might do to me now. They were probably asleep on their tartan-plaid sofas, where they had eaten microwaved dinners and watched multiple channels on their satellite dishes. I was the hunter now. The stillness of the land was my personal geography, the buggy trail a river of light. I passed by the first of the squatters' camps, a neat frame house with screened-in porch and freshly cut lawn. It was followed by a jungle of signs for fanciful roads and neighborhoods like Tar Pit Alley and Slant Pine Row. And then, just as I was beginning to think kindly of my inventive neighbors, the Mirees' compound with its wrecked school buses and open latrines came into view, a scene so dismal and offensive to the moral intelligence that not even morning could rescue it from what it was.

This was the routine I followed for three nights in a row—cutting the fence, a different section line each time; plodding down the darkened buggy trails; standing guard at the canvas house until dawn; and then walking back by way of the gatehouse. It was the middle of Holy Week. I didn't see a soul. But I felt vigorous and right in my calling. And then the wire-cutting, and my impersonation of the camouflage man, came to an end on Maundy Thursday, when I happened upon an accident, just after dark, on the highway to Lake Wales.

Two horses had escaped from their paddock and tried to cross the highway. One, a red roan, had been hit by a truck. The windshield of the truck was broken out, and blood and excrement smeared the dash. Tufts of horsehair were lodged in the windshield wipers, and the body of the horse looked unreal in the gathering headlights. Its eye had been gouged out, its belly ripped open, and the two hind legs were broken in such a way that the bone stuck out and shimmered, opalescent, like the still-living tissue it was. The horse itself was dead.

I pressed my shirt to the bloodied face of the truck driver, a black man who was worried about his wife back home. I had to admit it: There really was a need for fences. You could argue for years about who should be allowed inside or kept out. But fences served a purpose, and I had been wrong to cut the ones I had. So I resolved to let my obsession with River Ranch rest a while, a season at least, until I could regain my sense of proportion, but that's about the time the FBI showed up at my door in Birmingham.

In all, there were five men lined up on the front porch: two uniformed police officers; two beefy guys in civilian clothes, one white, one black; and a portly man in a red windbreaker. He was the one who claimed to be from the FBI. He asked if I was Dennis Covington. He asked if I owned a 1984 Jeep Cherokee. I answered yes to both questions.

"Do you know where your vehicle is now?"

I told him I thought I did. Then I glanced at the black guy next to him. This guy was muscular and wore faded, grease-stained jeans and a dusty crew-neck shirt. He looked as if he'd just crawled out from under a cattle car. I thought there were even pieces of straw in his hair. I figured he was the car thief they wanted me to identify.

"My Jeep is, or was, in central Florida," I said pointedly.

"In the middle of the woods," the black guy added with enough emphasis to let me know I had it all wrong; he wasn't a suspect, he was the Law.

"It was on my property," I said. "What's going on?"
The men just stared at me.

"Come on in," I said. I was glad Vicki and I had just had the inside of our house repainted—Berber carpet, ivory walls. In the living room, Vicki had hung framed photos of our families and the kids, and a couple of paintings by the Salvadoran artist Fernando Llort. These improvements made us appear more respectable than we would have a mere two weeks before, but I did remember with a pang of anxiety that there was an opened jar of mayonnaise on the counter in the kitchen.

Vicki, who had once been involved with an FBI agent and knew about these things, told me that every time agents went to make an arrest at a house where white trash lived, there was an opened jar of mayonnaise on the kitchen counter. I hoped these men weren't going to insist on seeing our kitchen.

I motioned for everyone to sit down. Nobody did but me. The man in the red windbreaker rocked forward on the balls of his feet. He had an unnaturally level gaze and rosy cheeks. Nothing about him said FBI except the eyes. He said agents from the bureau's office in central Florida had come across my Jeep and cabin in an unincorporated area of Polk County. Everything had been shot up.

"It looked like a war zone down there. They said it was like Beirut," he said. "We just stopped by to make sure you were alive."

I told them it was the third time my place had been shot up.

"What are these people so mad about?" the black guy asked.

"It's a land dispute," I said, and I could sense the men's interest wane. "It's my land, though. My father left it to me. I've had it surveyed. I've got the deed."

I said all this last part in a rush while the agent and policemen were easing themselves out the door. They'd gotten what they'd come for. The crazy dude with the shot-up Jeep and cabin was still in one piece, so there was nothing to investigate, no carpets to comb or fragments of bone to reassemble. The last one out, the black man in ordinary clothes, turned on the porch and said, "Hey, I'm glad you're all right. But you be careful down there in Florida. Those guys mean business."

"Wow!" Ashley said when I closed the door behind him. I'd forgotten she was home from school and had been listening to all this. "I can't wait to tell Mom the FBI came to our house to interrogate you!"

I couldn't wait to see Vicki's face, either. It seemed to me that a phone call from our local police precinct might have served just as well, but Vicki's FBI pal later told her the team was probably prepared for a hostage situation, a kidnapping with some kind of bloody resolution in the offing. If that was the case, I could see why the men seemed so disappointed as they hunched back across my lawn to their cars.

This time the Polk County sheriff's department dispatcher wanted me to meet the investigating officer at the scene of the crime.

"You don't seem to understand," I told her. "The FBI said my camp looked like a war zone. I am not going out there alone. This deputy is going to ride out there with me."

The dispatcher agreed, and I took some comfort in the fact that at least the sheriff's department was taking the incident seriously enough to visit the crime scene. The third officer was different from the others, older and more experienced than the first but more cautious in his comments than the second. He said he was a former homicide detective who had worked some of the most notorious murders in the county.

"How'd the FBI get involved in this?" he asked.

I told him I didn't know.

He drove his patrol car to the Hunt Club front gate and left it there, so Pete Edwards and everybody else would know something serious had occurred, and then he climbed into my truck and we headed for the land.

My CB crackled.

"Buckshot. Come in, Buckshot. This is Gate One. Do you read me?"

I told Peanut I read her.

"Buckshot, are you all right?" she asked. "I see you got the Law riding with you."

"I'm about the same as before."

"Be careful, son," she said.

"Ten-four, Gate One. Over and out."

This investigator seemed interested in every detail I could remember, anything about people who'd made specific threats. When I mentioned the Mirees, he simply pursed his lips—no tasteless jokes at their expense. No dismissing them, either. And when we came within sight of my camp, he whistled through his teeth.

It was a hard thing for me to look at. The Jeep had been stripped and gutted of everything that could be removed or burnt away. What hadn't been taken was strewn all over the field. The remaining carcass of the Jeep was riddled with bullet holes and had been crushed like an accordion, bent upon itself by some terrible force.

"They must have driven something into it," the investigator said. "Swamp buggy, I reckon. What about the cabin?"

I didn't think it possible for the cabin to look much worse than it had the last time, but it did. More bullet holes, more fancy knife work, and this time, in the same spot where the dead armadillo had been, someone had placed my orange hunting cap.

The investigator nodded slowly when he noticed that detail, and then he motioned for us to get back into the truck. There wasn't any more to be done here, his gesture seemed to suggest.

"It looks like a pretty open and shut case to me," he said as we lurched back through the mudholes toward the Hunt Club's main gate. "These people would like to see you dead."

I figured I could have told him that.

And then the investigator launched into a story about the worst murder scene he had ever come across. This was up in Lake City, Florida, he said. A man had complained once too often about how his wife cooked his eggs. So on one particular morning, after serving up the third pair of eggs that her husband rejected, the wife took her skillet and proceeded to bash in his head.

"I mean, she didn't stop when he was dead," the investigator said. "She kept pounding him with that skillet. There was blood and brains and pieces of hairy scalp all over the kitchen walls and floor. It was not a pretty sight. But, you know, the wife was cool as a cucumber when we got her down to headquarters. Said it was that time of the month, and she just wasn't feeling right."

That was the moment I began to lose hope. The story, you see, of the wife and the skillet—I'd heard it before, all over the South. I'd done plenty of true crime reporting for newspapers and magazines, and the minute an investigator started telling that story, I knew to put my pen and notebook away. It was an apocryphal tale, a kind of small-town lawman's "alligators in the sewer" myth. It was another way of saying, I've got better things to do, buddy-roo. It was a way of saying, Why don't you go back home where you belong? Maybe then, you wouldn't get shot at so much.

Nobody was going to be arrested for destroying my camp. And there was no way I could ever bring my family down to our property at River Ranch for a fun-filled wilderness vacation. Cowboy songs around the old campfire were out of the question now.

I'd come to the end of a certain part of my journey. I had made myself notorious all right. It was my land, more than six acres of it now, but there was nothing I could do with it unless I crossed a line of risk I wasn't prepared to assume. The reason I had come to Florida was starting to blur in my mind. The only resolution I could imagine was to invite Pete Edwards or one of the Mirees out to my land on the pretext of talking things out and then, like Rory Calhoun or Kirk Douglas, pull back my leather vest to reveal the holstered revolver and say, "Draw!" High Noon under the Florida sun.

But was this really the inheritance Dad intended to leave me? Maybe wrestling that Florida land from the bad guys wasn't what he had in mind after all. The dream my father had carried to his grave must have been broader than that; dangerous, but in a different way; more significant perhaps. I'd have to think this one through. Here I was, coming up on Dad's age when he used the profits from the sale of Covington Groceries to buy his piece of River Ranch Acres, but I still didn't know exactly what he had in mind when he left it so explicitly to me . . . unless he thought he might be preparing me for a career in blue-collar crime and/or real estate.

Land Fever

The more I read about the land scams of the 1960s and 1970s, the more convinced I became that there were thousands of "paper subdivisions" like River Ranch Acres hidden in courthouse records across the breadth of America. Any one or two of these paper subdivisions might be the mother lode—scenic, unspoiled, and uncontested land that I could pick up for back taxes, lot by contiguous lot, the way I had picked up the two pieces adjoining Dad's land in Florida. It was a strategy my real estate books called "plottage."

If I assembled the lots into parcels large enough for recreational purposes (the site of a wilderness retreat, say, like my shot-up place in Florida), I could sell the parcels to members of the swelling baby boom for a healthy profit. I'd be a Rosen brother in reverse!

Subdivisions that seemed scandalously remote from amenities and employers in the 1960s might be perfectly suited to the wired and wireless generation of the new century, a generation already accustomed to the idea of choosing where they wanted to live and then working out of there, rather than choosing their line of work and moving to a place that had jobs in the field.

For members of this generation, a wind-blown desert might be their Shangri-la. They might prefer the wail of coyotes to the chatter of socialites at a nearby country club. My God, they were already throwing each other off cliffs with or without parachutes and snow skiing on *boards*. Their idea of a vacation was nowhere near visiting Clearwater or St. Petersburg, but maybe climbing Mt. Rainier during a lightning storm or photographing a volcanic eruption in progress on an island accessible by ferry only during the other half of the year.

The demographics were on my side. By the year 2010, there would be only 7 million American men my age (60–64). But there would be 10 million in their fifties; 15 million in their forties; and more than 20 million in their cliff-jumping, ski-boarding, paragliding, volcano-diving thirties. City and suburbia would be passé. Bankrupt land development schemes in the middle of nowhere would be the rage.

One of the payoffs would be land of my own—scenic, remote, uncontested land. And there would be, of course, an additional financial windfall. I could be like the guy on the television infomercial who claimed to be making a killing in tax-forfeited land.

I was deadly serious about all this, and the Internet teemed with helpful sites. "Fun and Profits in Tax

Forfeited Lands!" trumpeted one of them. A form to order manuals for each state was provided. None of these sites used the term "paper subdivision," but I found at least one company that, every two or three months, auctioned off hundreds of individual lots in subdivisions that must have been very much like River Ranch Acres. These subdivisions were in the western states, the real west, as opposed to River Ranch's synthetic variety. I learned there were paper subdivisions all over California and Nevada, some the work of Leonard Rosen before he died. Others were located around Deming, New Mexico; Malheur County, Oregon; Iron County, Utah; and along the Salmon River in the remotest reaches of Idaho. According to the auction brochures, lots in these subdivisions could be bought for pennies on the dollar of their original purchase price.

There was one problem.

I didn't have the pennies even to attend one of these auctions, much less place bids on any of the aforementioned lots. In fact, the IRS was about to place a lien on my house in Birmingham for failure to pay back taxes. With that in the offing, how was I supposed to buy tax-forfeited land two thousand miles away? Somebody in Wisconsin was probably studying how to buy mine.

Fortunately, though, I had been reading my real estate books very carefully, and I had learned that there were no impossibilities in real estate, only challenges to be met and overcome. The solution to my dilemma was a corporate structure called "the limited partnership."

In a limited partnership, only some of the investors cough up real money. These investors, the "limited" partners, have no say in how their investment is managed, but they are compensated for this risk by not being held liable for debts incurred above their investment, should the entire enterprise fail.

The "general" partners, on the other hand, are liable for corporate losses. They are the managers, the schemers who dream up the idea of, say, assembling tax-forfeited lots in paper subdivisions out west somewhere. But they don't put up a dime of their own money. And they share, according to prior agreement, in the profits of the partnership, just as though they had invested money. Their investment is in time and expertise.

Just the ticket for me and my friend Jim Neel, who, always a good sport, played along with me on the idea. As general partners, we could assemble the parcels from lots bought at auction or tax sales; drill our own wells; and erect the cabins, each heated by a wood or propane stove and powered by a windmill and modest solar array. Then we'd leave a hand-painted sign that read, say, "6 acres with cabin for sale. Call Jim or Dennis" and give one of our Alabama phone numbers. To a prospective buyer, we'd seem like two ordinary dumb Southern guys, hunters or tree huggers, who had gotten in over our heads by building a cabin we'd never use, but in reality that cabin would be one of many in paper subdivisions all over the place. The name of our enterprise would be "Call Jim or Dennis, Inc."

We could double our money with each sale.

And since we were general partners, we wouldn't be putting up the initial capital. That would come from the limited partners, who would be, let's see, the usual suspects: our friends who were doctors, lawyers, and dentists. A handful, yes, but enough.

Unfortunately, Vicki found the list of potential investors and my carefully written form letter before I had the opportunity to mail it to our doctor, lawyer, and dentist friends.

"What?" she said. "You're going to do what?"

I explained there was a perfectly rational idea at work in this.

She tore up the letter and told me never to mention the term "real estate" in front of her again.

I don't think Vicki understood at the time that my longing for a quick buck might have been a genetic disorder, like my father's color-blindness—some defect the Anglo-Irish had brought over with them when they settled in the Appalachians: fast money for little work. Every family in our part of the country seems to have stories about successes or failures in this regard.

Those armadillos, for instance—the great money-making scheme that Bert and I had hatched in 1962. We could have quadrupled our money, had we not been depending on the integrity of Mr. Kenneth Foote, another redneck like ourselves, who couldn't be bothered to find any armadillos in Texas until the rain came and forced them from their burrows.

Bert and I lost money on that one. But we made money on a smaller scheme, selling snake-trap plans for fifty cents apiece. We invented the design of the trap, placed an ad in *Fur, Fish, and Game*, and made copies of the plans on a gelatinous ink tray (this was long before Xerox, mind you). I don't know how many orders we got, but the number was more than we deserved, because we never actually *built* the snake trap. We just drew up *plans* for it. I do believe the trap would have worked, at least theoretically. But the proof was left to the customers who bought the plans and constructed the traps from them. All I know is, nobody ever complained to us about not being able to catch snakes using the trap we designed.

Bert and I also made a little money catching salamanders and newts for a Dr. Shackleford at the local university. He was doing medical research (I don't like to think what kind) and had bought a number of our armadillos. Among other unusual characteristics (bouncing, for instance, is their prime means of defense), armadillos are the only animals that always bear identical quadruplets, making them ideal subjects for investigations concerning cell division and, therefore, cancer research. In addition, they are known to be carriers of leprosy.

We couldn't continue to supply Dr. Shackleford with armadillos, though, for the obvious reason that we were losing money in the armadillo trade, but Shackleford made it clear that he could use all the salamanders and newts we could provide. I don't know what their special qualifications for medical research might be. Despite the fact that my mother had always wanted me to go into medical research (and who knows but that all this might have qualified), the salamanders and newts were strictly business.

So we harvested as many as we could from the creeks that coursed down Ruffner Mountain, and then we retired from that line of work. Our motives, despite the snake-trap plans, had been more or less pure. It seems inevitable in retrospect, though, that Bert would become a doctor and that the obsession to claim my inheritance, those two and a half acres at River Ranch, Florida, would result in yet another crazed attempt to make a pile of money in something I knew absolutely nothing about. This, by the way, is the redneck formula for success.

So with visions of tax-forfeited land dancing in my head, I applied for a job as a writer-in-residence at Boise State University in Idaho. It was only a six-week position, but it paid well and I'd have to teach only one course. When the job was offered, I didn't think twice. I told the chairman at BSU that I'd seen Boise from the air once and felt a kinship to the terrain, a combination of desert, river plain, and forested mountains. I also knew that Boise had been an important stop for wagon trains on the Oregon Trail. One of Dad's favorite TV programs had been *Wagon Train*. He also liked its spin-off, *Rawhide*, with the boyish Clint Eastwood and that classic intro music sung by

Frankie Laine: "Rollin', rollin', rollin' . . . keep them dogies rollin' . . . "

And of course there were those paper subdivisions along the Salmon River.

That January, Laura and I piled our gear into the bed of the pickup and headed west. I took just about everything I owned, including my well-drilling equipment, GPS, and maps of every description and size. I had plat maps of the paper subdivisions along the Salmon River, Bureau of Land Management maps, topo maps, and an enormous geologic map of the entire state of Idaho.

Laura was ten years old. I would turn fifty later that year. Each morning, we started our day with Jackson Brown's "Running on Empty," followed by Laura's favorite tape, *Middle of Nowhere*, by the three teenage heartthrobs called Hanson. We even made a point of directing our route through Tulsa, Oklahoma, Hanson's hometown, and though we couldn't find the house where the brothers lived, we did stumble across a souvenir store that had life-size posters of Isaac, Taylor, and especially, as Laura reminds me, Zac.

We climbed into the truck again and continued westward. This was the road trip I had always wished I'd made with my father: the millions of migrating birds we saw, flocks that stretched from horizon to horizon and seemed to reverse nap, like velvet rubbed the wrong way, each time they adjusted course; the sunsets and sunrises; the endless stretch of highway across plains and prairie that failed to produce the World's Largest Prairie Dog as promised. The gimmick was an enormous concrete statue of a prairie dog, but it and the advertised menagerie of western wildlife were closed for the season.

We encountered no one for mile upon mile upon mile, and after a time, the marvel of flat land and overarching sky began to fade. Laura fell asleep, and it wasn't until we had climbed up out of the plains and faced the front range of the Colorado Rockies—a hard, dry snow pelting the roadway—that Laura woke up, and I was able to utter the words every American parent of a certain age must ache to say to a daughter or son: "Toto, I have a feeling we're not in Kansas anymore."

The one trip Dad and I did make alone together had been to Huntsville, Alabama, a few years before he died. He wanted to see the space shuttle *Columbia,* and so did I. I hoped we'd see my brother Scotty there, too, but then I remembered he no longer worked at the Marshall Space Flight Center.

Scotty had been a test stand engineer on the Jupiter project, the rocket that carried Alan Shepherd and John Glenn and the other Mercury astronauts into space, but when Scotty saw the crunch coming after the failed Apollo mission, he left the space program and became chief engineer for an aluminum company in Decatur. He still lived in the rarefied atmosphere of his imagination, dreaming of space stations and booster rockets powerful enough to take men beyond the edges of the solar system. He imagined building airplanes in his garage and even earned his pilot's license. He gave my father the only airplane ride of his life. That's what I remember most about Scotty, other than his integrity and generosity. He loved to fly.

As he aged, Dad himself had given in to a fascination with space, its magnitude and mystery. The subject did not seem to displace his interest in Christianity. It simply reaffirmed his belief that "conventional Christian theology" was a contradiction in terms. The idea that a supernatural intelligence had made the universe, for instance, was far from conventional, no matter how many other cultures and religions echoed the theme. "The more we learn about the universe," Dad would say, holding his coffee spoon aloft for emphasis, "the more reason we have to worship God." And then, in a characteristic non sequitur intended, I think, to deflate his own pomposity, he would point the spoon at me and say, "How would you like to worship a god with nine heads?"

Then he'd answer his own question. "That would make for some interesting defugalties, don't you think?"

Dad taught Sunday School lessons about cosmology to his friends in the Wesley Fellowship Class and tried to interest Mom and me in photographs of deep space objects—crab nebula, twin dwarfs, and soupy oceans of interstellar gas. Mother pretended to be able to see the photographs. I feigned interest, too. It was not until I saw the night sky from the desert floor, without a single competing light source in view, that I started to appreciate this key part of my father's fascination with the ocean and the west. It had to do with space. The wider the vista, the more at home he seemed to be. It was a trait that Scotty and I inherited from him.

Laura stayed with me in Idaho for the first week. We had an efficiency apartment at the Boise River Inn. At dawn, we fed cracked corn to the wood ducks, mallards, and Canada geese who swam in the creek outside our door. The creek joined the Boise River a few hundred yards west, and we'd walk along the banks of the river to the university or to the city parks or museums. Sometimes, Laura rollerbladed ahead of me, then came back to circle me in figure eights. Boyish and blond, she was perfectly at home in Idaho. The air was clean, the river swift and clear, and in the distance we could see the snow-covered peaks of the Boise Front. We even tried snow skiing at Bogus Basin, north of the city, a first for both of us. Laura had natural talent. "You could be another Picabo Street," one of the instructors told her.

Emboldened by Laura's prowess on the beginner slope, we took the lift adjoining it, thinking that this run would represent the next level of difficulty. In the course of our long ascent to the top of the mountain, as the trees shrank smaller and smaller beneath us until they disappeared into the morning mist, I had the feeling we'd made a mistake. When we reached the top, I knew we had. The run was a black diamond. But there was no way down except on skis. The slope seemed to drop at an impossible angle into the mist. I lasted about thirty seconds before flipping head over heels into the snow. I heard my left knee snap and knew something had gone terribly wrong. The ski patrol wrapped me in blankets and zipped me into a canvas bag before they transported me down the mountain in a sled.

"Is it a body?" I heard someone ask along the route.

Laura skied behind one of the patrol members, a woman who assumed that Laura was experienced. Why else would her father have taken her onto a black diamond slope? My ten-year-old Alabama girl had conquered a black diamond on her second day of snow skiing. A legend in the making.

Not so for her father.

After having my knee packed in ice, I drove us back to Boise that day, learning later that I had torn my anterior cruciate ligament, one of the most common ski injuries. The condition would require surgery back in Birmingham, where the surgeon would have to graft a tendon from the front of my leg into the middle of my knee; a year of physical therapy would follow. For the time being, though, I just iced and kept it elevated.

No more skiing for me. No rambling deep into the Idaho woods as I'd planned. But I got plenty of exercise, both at the sports medicine clinic at Boise State and on my walks along the river to class. And I had time to indulge my newest obsession, the hunt for land in Idaho that would meet the criteria I'd set in order to begin my ascent as a real estate magnate.

I spread the enormous geologic map of Idaho on the floor of my apartment and drew a circle with a radius of fifty miles around the city of Boise, one of the fastest-growing urban centers in the country. I was looking for a wild, scenic area that adjoined Bureau of Land Management holdings or a national forest. This land would have to be accessible year-round and would have to be located on an alluvial plain geologically conducive to the finding of subsurface water at a reasonable depth.

These criteria ruled out the paper subdivisions in central and northern Idaho. They were much too far from Boise, plagued by deep winter snows, and atop terrain impossible for an amateur well driller like me.

The few places on the map that seemed to fit my criteria, I circled in pencil. I knew the ones closest to Boise would be too expensive. Those spots were already being transformed into residential subdivisions. Finding privately held land in other parts of the state was a challenge. The best candidates were on the Camas Prairie near the town of Fairfield, and south of the Snake River in the immense, largely empty Owyhee Desert.

In an Idaho guidebook, I had seen photos of both places, the Camas Prairie with its riot of wildflowers and the Owyhee Desert with its sagebrush silvered by morning frost. Behind both of these flattened foregrounds loomed snow-covered mountains. I liked the Owyhee Mountains best. They seemed close and voluptuous, mountains that men might worship and ultimately lose themselves in. The mountains above the

Camas Prairie were more predictable. Prettified skiers' mountains. I'd later learn that Hollywood actor Bruce Willis had bought the previously family-owned ski run on Soldier Mountain, the signature peak of the range, and planned to develop it into a premier ski resort. So that was another factor. Land around Fairfield wouldn't be cheap.

Owyhee County, though, was nowhere near becoming a resort of any kind. Murphy, its county seat, had only seventy-five residents, and there were unlikely to be many more in the future, because, with few exceptions, the land fronting the Owyhees was owned by the Bureau of Land Management. Privately owned land was rare and, unless it happened to be irrigated from the Snake River, bone dry. I did note, though, that there were snatches of alluvial plain in the Owyhee Desert, particularly in one valley where two creeks—Bates and Pickett—converged. The convergence of the creeks was about seven miles west of a dot on the map called Oreana. That was the exact spot I circled on my geologic map: privately held land in an alluvial plain, with a view of the Owyhee Mountains.

I studied land advertisements in the Sunday *Idaho Statesman*, but nothing caught my full attention until, over dinner at a Mexican restaurant in Nampa, I saw an ad in the local *Wooden Nickel*. It was for forty acres in Owyhee County, near Oreana. I called Silver Dollar Realty for directions. The forty had already been sold, the agent said, but there were another ten acres at the same location, a piece of level pasture that fronted Pickett Creek by what he called "Thelma's place."

I drove to Oreana on a Sunday afternoon, passing the spot where the guidebook photograph of the Owyhee Mountains must have been taken. The land was as lonely and spectacular as it had appeared in the photo. What couldn't be captured in the still photograph were the subtleties of color and movement. Sagebrush, for instance, comes in every possible shade of green, blue, brown and gray. The sand, mesas, and arroyos of the desert are composed of infinite variations on yellow and red. And this description doesn't even take into account the effects of the sun at its various angles, the shifting clouds, sudden rain showers, or other atmospheric conditions that turn the entire sky into a prism of special effects.

The turnoff to Oreana appeared to head straight across the desert toward the Owyhees, but after a couple of miles, it dipped and fell into an agricultural valley, pasture land dotted with cows. On the left was a well-drilling company, and then the Oreana Bar and Grill. On the right stretched pasture and the Owyhee Mountains; tacked to a fence was a hand-painted sign: "Oreana City Centre," the sign read, "pop. 7, maybe 8."

This was the valley I'd circled on the geologic map, and as I followed the real estate agent's directions— bearing right on Bates Creek Road and following it past isolated farmhouses until the gravel gave way to dirt—I realized I was headed toward the convergence point of the two creeks.

The miles uncoiled slowly, the farmhouses vanishing one by one until all I could see was the earth and sky, the line of bare cottonwoods along the creek, a piebald horse in the pasture to my left, a pheasant breaking for cover in the sandy hills to my right. The road continued to deteriorate until finally I passed through the blue gate with its cattle guard, curled around a curve in the road, and saw the spot where the creeks came together, a fine rushing stream at this time of year, and the nearby barn and farmhouse that must have been Thelma's place.

Thelma Rumsey greeted me at the door with a sly smile that seemed to suggest she knew I was coming, although I couldn't see how. Her face was weathered by sun and wind, her pale blue eyes unfathomable.

"You're the first car to come down this road in two weeks," she said, and then she added that she liked it that way. She'd always lived at the end of the road.

I explained to Thelma what I was doing there, and she showed me the ten-acre parcel that was for sale. Like the agent had said, it was pasture, and it did touch one of the creeks, Pickett Creek, on its south end. But the land didn't have a view of the mountains, and for that reason, I knew I wouldn't be making an offer—that, and the fact that I didn't have any money.

"What do you do for a living?" Thelma asked.

I told her I was a visiting professor at Boise State and that I wrote.

"I'm just a horse woman, but now and again I scribble something down. Some people might call it poetry," she said. "Come on in."

The farmhouse was actually a trailer that Thelma's ranching partner, Bob Vansickel, had clad in rough-sawn lumber. He had added a long, wraparound porch of the same material, extended the roof, and disguised the trailer's windows to give the effect of a rustic, cozy ranch house. Indeed, it had become that. A fire hissed in the wood-burning stove in the living room. The end table beside the easy chair was piled high with *American Horseman* magazines and catalogues advertising Native American blankets and crafts.

"Bob's a full-blooded Sioux and the best horse man in three states," Thelma said, and she pointed out the photos on the desk and wall, shots of thoroughbreds in the winner's circle, with trainers, owners, and well-wishers standing on either side of the animal. One person would be holding flowers, another the bronze cup. From the dress of the people and the clarity of the camera's focus, I guessed the photos were at least thirty years old.

Also adorning the walls were a stuffed pronghorn antelope head and depictions of typically western scenes—a coyote yapping from the top of a snowy hill in the desert; a print of an Indian warrior atop his paint pony, both in battle dress; and calendar art from feed and veterinary companies, most depicting gorgeous blondes in Levi's and cowboy boots.

"Those boys right there," Thelma said, indicating a cowboy calendar with a glossy of two teenagers leaning against a barn, "are from my place at Silver Lake. Nice kids, both of them."

Thelma poured us coffee, which we drank at the kitchen table, the high clear light of March pouring in on us. It would be a while before I understood that Thelma Rumsey's specialty was caring for men down on their luck. She had been married once to a drunk who had mistreated her and scared her by firing his shotgun into the air. "I figured he was going to blow me away," she said. She took care of this husband for as long as she could, but when she saw one of them was going to die imminently and realized she didn't want it to be her, she put the man in a veterans hospital and filed for divorce. Sure enough, his liver got him not long afterward.

But with a husband like that for more than twenty years, Thelma had mined her capacity for taking care of people, and so she was always on the lookout, particularly for men who had brought themselves down in some careless or despicable way. Men, I would come to realize, like me.

But I didn't know that yet, of course. I didn't know that she'd pretty much raised herself in the emptiness of eastern Oregon, with a black pony as her only companion. I didn't know she had attended college and wanted to be a journalist, until World War II came along, and she had to return to the ranch and milk cows instead. Thelma's hands were the smallest in her family, so that's how milking became her specialty.

If it hadn't been for horses, she might have fallen into despair over her broken ambitions. But horses, and her love of the land, opened up the world to Thelma in the same way the men's war had closed it. Horses became both her vocation and avocation. And it is unlikely that any mere journalistic assignment could have caused her eyes to moisten with so much pride and nostalgia as they did over the time she rode Appaloosas with Chief Joseph's son, and they won a long-ago pairs competition.

She would tell me those stories on another day. What Thelma wanted now was for me to get a good look at the Owyhee Mountains from her porch, so we drained our coffee and went outside. The mountains seemed very near and very white. A breeze stirred. I took a deep breath.

"That air came straight from Alaska," Thelma said. "It's never been breathed before."

She pointed to a notch in the mountains, to the left of the highest peak. "That's where this creek begins. It's a different world up there." And she told me about the stands of juniper and the alpine meadows, the elk herd and bighorn sheep.

I asked if there were mountain lions.

"Cougars? Up there? Sure. The other day, the survey-ors saw one down here at the Narrows. It was drinking from the creek."

A horse whinnied, and I looked toward the corral. One of Thelma's Aussie cow-herding dogs was crouched in front of a large golden horse, a dark gray one with a

stippled back, and a chestnut with an injured leg.
Soundlessly, the dog maneuvered to get a better angle on
them.

"That's Bob's palomino," she said, "and my old girl.
The one with the bandaged leg is a new one of Bob's.
He's at an auction right now. Thinks he can pick up a
brood mare, but I told him that's not what we need. We
need another good cow horse. As soon as the snow
melts, they'll be driving the cows to summer pasture."

"Who will?" I asked.

"Bob. The other ranchers and hands. They'll follow
the creek through the Narrows there and up into the
mountains. It's dangerous work. The footing's real bad
right after the melt."

"A roundup?" I said. "Like in the movies?"

Thelma looked at me out of the corner of her eye.
"That's right. Kind of. There's not much money in
ranching these days, but us old-timers, we're holding
on."

I imagined dust rising from hundreds of hooves, the
yapping of cow dogs, and the slapping of leather saddles
and boots. The cowboys were faceless—I didn't know
yet what Bob Vansickel looked like, but I saw a man I
assumed was him on the massive palomino. They were
preparing to drive the cattle toward the mountains,
along the creek and through the Narrows, where they
would be watched by yellow-eyed cats; past the sluices
of abandoned gold claims; the wagon ruts from the great
migration westward; the petroglyphs scratched into

canyon walls by men not that much different from themselves, men hallucinating out of physical hunger or spiritual ecstasy, men possessed and driven by need.

That's when I saw my father as a young rancher on horseback, under the cottonwoods by the creek. Dark-headed and sharp-featured, his lariat at his side, he was watching the dogs steer the cattle toward the Narrows. His eyes were grave, but his thin lips curled in a smile.

I carried that vision back with me to Birmingham—the notion that even at the beginning of a new century, in a country that was for the most part technologically driven and divorced from the land, it was possible to live a simple, vigorous life on the edge of the western frontier. My obsession with River Ranch Acres was pointing me now to Thelma's place, with its horses, cow dogs, desert, and mountains, a life that I know my father romanticized but one that he also must have thought could be his, especially about the time he reached my age.

Why else would he have bought land, sight unseen, in a Florida real estate development with a western theme?

Coyote Point

The following winter, I placed a second call to Silver Dollar Realty in Idaho. "Any other parcels in the area for sale?" I asked John Gabica, the Basque agent who had made a career out of being neighborly.

"I can't believe you called today," he said. "There's a thirty-acre parcel that's just gone on the market. It hasn't even been advertised yet, but we've had people calling anyway." He said the land adjoined Thelma Rumsey's place. There was a piece of dry pasture with it, but most of the acreage spread across a series of sandy hills to a plateau with a panoramic view.

"There's no crick," John warned me, although he said water could probably be reached within 150 feet down by Thelma's. The best thing was that the price was only $1,000 an acre, with possible owner financing.

"Are you sure it has a view of the mountains?" I asked him.

John paused. "Why, yes," he said, but the hesitation in his voice worried me a bit.

I persuaded him to hold the land long enough for me to get to Idaho and take a look. When I did, it was night. Thelma's dogs were barking in the distance. I climbed the first ridge doubtfully, but when I reached the top, the snow-covered Owyhees spilled out of the night sky. And there were higher, flatter ridges behind me. The land had a view, all right. I wanted it. I wanted it all.

The next day, I was back at dawn, to check out the highest point on the land, a potential cabin site. From the edge of the plateau, a finger of land jutted out over a draw. A coyote was sitting on that finger of land watching for prey in the valley below. He disappeared before I could release my breath, a gray ghost in the mauve and magical light. I knew then I would call my land Coyote Point, to include the spit where he had been sitting and wherever on the ridge I chose to build a cabin.

In the meantime, I watched the mountains, snow blowing in sheets across the escarpments and draws. There were the three billowing folds of the Cinnabars, and War Eagle Mountain, somewhere in the valleys of which lay the ghost town of Silver City. Mountains to the left and right as far as I could see. Behind me the desert stretched down to the Snake River plain and beyond that for ninety more miles or so until the mountains rose again, this time all the way to the blinding white of Mt. Baldy, the centerpiece of Sun Valley. If I stood at the highest point on the plateau, I could see no sign of human habitation in any direction, a hundred miles or more of nothing but land and sky, scattered trees, sagebrush, rocks.

Back down in the valley, while trying to find the southeast corner of the land that I already was thinking of as mine, I came upon Thelma's partner, Bob Vansickel, on his huge palomino. Bob was moving cattle down the creek bed to a more sheltered spot, where the newborn calves could be better protected from coyotes, who had killed two calves the night before. Bob was dressed in his full range gear—boots and spurs, leather chaps and vest, a dusty chamois shirt and cowboy hat; the signature blue scarf of his spread, Kamaloops Ranch, was knotted around his neck.

"My God," I said. "You look like John Wayne."

Bob shrugged and gazed down the valley, where his cow dog was urging a stubborn heifer through the brush.

"Just another day in Idaho," he said.

Idaho. The name held mystery and promise. Forget the shot-up canvas house at River Ranch, the boxes of excrement, the hog intestines, the crushed Jeep. Forget the paper subdivisions near Deming, New Mexico, and in Malheur County, Oregon. Forget even the ones along the Salmon River in what was, in ways, another state. My dream of assembling tax-forfeited lots into parcels large enough for recreational use had morphed, thanks to my real estate books and the vision of Kamaloops

Ranch, into a less complicated, time tested, and more in-
stantly gratifying strategy—the use of installment buying
to "leverage" a spectacular return on a modest investment in raw land in Owyhee County, Idaho. Borrowed
money would be the tool. Appreciation and timing
would be the method. According to my calculations, if I
bought the thirty acres from John Gabica for $30,000,
with a down payment of $3,000 and the balance spread
over fifteen years at 10 percent interest, I could, after
four years, sell the land for $60,000 and reap a crisp
128 percent return on my investment.

More important, I would have redeemed my inheritance.

What the Hunt Club had denied me, as a practical
matter, in the west of my father's imagination, I would
claim for him in the real west. Whereas Dad's investment had been in grossly overpriced and unsurveyed
land baited with the false promise of ultimate development, I would be investing in cheap land with deeded,
year-round access; proximity to ground water; thousands of adjoining acres protected by the federal government; magnificent views—it couldn't fail. I could have
my cake and eat it—an investment, but also an isolated
and wind-swept retreat for my and my family's use.

By this time, it had occurred to me that the least expensive and most meaningful way to put a cabin on the
land was to dismantle the workshop my father had built
in his backyard in Birmingham in 1973, ship it in pieces
to Idaho, and erect it again on the very spot where the

coyote had sat watching for prey in the valley below. There was symmetry here. Dad, I thought, would approve.

The workshop, sixteen by sixteen feet, was built from a design Dad found in *Popular Science*. It had a high-pitched back roof and clerestory windows down to a lower roof in front, a style called contemporary even back then. Dad modified the design by erecting an interior wall that divided the space into two rooms. Each had its own door to the outside. Dad finished the room on the right, installing heat and a telephone; this room was to be my mother's art studio. The unfinished room on the left housed Dad's table saw and other woodworking tools. There, he planned to build frames for my mother's canvases. Both spaces, though narrow, benefited from the clerestory windows' light.

This was the summer I worked with Dad at a small company that sold, rented, and repaired forklifts. Dad was the office manager, and I helped him in shipping and receiving. Occasionally, I'd get to drive one of the company trucks to a client's warehouse or factory and do minor repairs on an ailing forklift.

When I returned, I would see Dad standing at the counter in shipping and receiving, his bulbous nose and endless forehead silhouetted in a clear light swimming with dust motes. Dad would be holding aloft a part for one of the forklifts, contraptions he knew next to nothing about, except that their pieces had names and prices, sizes and weights, and could be shipped and received from nearly any place in the United States, and then neatly catalogued, stored, and sold to corporate customers at a profit, just like slices of bologna or cheese at Covington Groceries so many years before.

Dad was a demanding boss, in that he expected accuracy and promptness, but he never implied I was guilty of either. He endured my fumblings with patience and an amused, detached irony, as though he and I shared a secret the others at the company could never grasp. The secret was no secret at all, except in terms of what lay beneath the surface of the obvious. I was his son—and there's a mystery in that.

As much as I enjoyed being with Dad every workday, I was grateful that he assumed we would lunch separately. It was his way of reminding me, I think, that he did not take my company for granted. Perhaps I had other people I would rather eat lunch with. I didn't. Nor, I think, did he. But we parted for lunch every noon, then returned to each other to finish out the day. It transformed the two times we did eat together (fish sandwiches from McDonald's) into minor celebrations.

Uncle Brother and Uncle Howard helped Dad frame the workshop. I painted the outside an institutional green. Then, in the fall, I left for graduate school in Iowa.

When I moved back to Birmingham two years later, I found that Dad had indeed been constructing frames in his side of the workshop. Nearly every weekend, he and

Mother filled his orange Astre station wagon with her primitive oil paintings, mostly still lifes and landscapes but with striking touches—gyrating birds, for instance, against a crimson sky. They hauled these to art shows at area malls and hospitals. Mom always underpriced her competition, but she had the unsettling habit of giving her paintings as gifts to friends and relatives, and then taking them back, literally off the walls, in order to sell them at upcoming shows.

To my knowledge, Mom never actually painted in her side of Dad's workshop, but that didn't seem to surprise him. He had constructed the workshop as a duplex, but I believe the room on the right was simply an offering to my mother in an attempt to keep her from giving him trouble about the project. Dad had wanted to build a little house in his backyard, and he was willing to give up half the space in it to mollify Mother. I don't think he believed for one minute that Mother would make use of the space, so maybe it's unfair to characterize the room as a gift. But for the sake of argument, I say it was and have extrapolated thus: Mother had difficulty accepting, and giving, gifts.

Often, Mother's gift giving was intended to be instructional. One Christmas, she gift-wrapped a doll for my niece, Judy, who was just shy of four years old. Judy tore into the package with predictable expectation but burst into tears when she saw her gift. It was a doll from her past, one of her old ones that she had left at Mother's house. From Mother's point of view, the lesson must have been clear: Be satisfied with what you have and take better care of it. To the rest of us, the lesson was equally clear: Grandma's a nut; watch out for her.

Mom also loved to recycle gifts in less dramatic form. You might, for instance, discover a package under the Christmas tree that contained a tie and shirt you'd given your brother for his birthday the previous summer. Or you might find an item that had already been given to you for your birthday in the fall. You hadn't worn it yet, though, so it was fair game to be reinvented as a Christmas present.

As a result, my favorite holiday was Halloween, because with Halloween, the notion of tricks or treats had been institutionalized. Tricks at Halloween were part of the fun. Tricks at Christmas were not.

The summer after Dad finished his workshop, I had lunch with him and Mother at a rundown restaurant in Five Points South, the center of bohemian life in Birmingham, if such a place can be imagined. How the discussion over turnip greens, squash, and black-eyed peas arrived at the topic of homosexuality, I will never know. Perhaps I was just spoiling for a fight. But I do remember that at some point during the meal, I felt obliged to explain to my mother and father that Jesus was a homosexual.

Mom and Dad didn't take this well.

"The only person who ever called John beloved was John himself," my father said. He had anticipated the course of my logic, which was that the disciple John appeared to have an unseemly close relationship with the son of God.

But Dad's argument was lost on me; I had made the announcement for its shock value rather than its merit. Dad's words were also lost on my mother, who had disappeared from the table entirely and fled the restaurant in tears.

Dad and I looked at each another solemnly, both of us taking stock of the situation. I'd committed an outrageous act of sacrilege. Dad had defended Jesus admirably. Now what?

"Let me ask you just one thing," Dad said. He put his fork down and stared at it, as he was prone to do in the middle of a meal. I'd inherited this trait from him.

"How do they do it?" he said. And he looked past me toward the street outside. "I mean, how do men have sex with other men?"

I thought he was joking until I remembered that he had been born in 1912, the year the *Titanic* sank. He had spent his life among a generation of men who did not, as a rule, discuss the mechanics of homosexual love. Whatever these mechanics happened to be, Dad did not think them appropriate. On the other hand, he had never been opposed to learning something new.

I told him what I'd gathered about the subject, and he seemed grateful for the information. But then he turned the conversation back to Jesus and his beloved, John.

"You should try not to startle your mother like that," he said. "You know how she feels about sex and religion. You know what she's been through."

I knew, all right. Mom's father, a private detective, had died of syphilis at the state mental hospital.

"He was educated up north," my mother used to tell us. "In Tennessee," she would add, as though this northern exposure explained his predilection for women other than the one he'd married.

It must have been a hard environment in my mother's home, what with the poverty my grandfather Russell's occupation inflicted on the family, and the occasional surprises, like the dead man who showed up one morning in their front yard.

There was no Christmas in the Russell household one year. And my mother remembers a time when the only food item in the house was a chicken neck, with which my grandmother made a pot of soup. Mom and her older sister were the only children.

"You're the smart but plain one," my grandfather would say to Mom's sister. "And you're the pretty but stupid one," he would say to Mother.

What this background had to do with Jesus' sexual preferences eluded me at the time. To Dad, my mother's struggle growing up demanded a degree of protectiveness that I believe Mom could have done without, because it resulted in a paternalism on my father's part that may have smothered, rather than cultivated, her considerable gifts.

That she was difficult to live with—even methodical and ruthless at times—can't be denied. But my mother was a visual artist who started painting late in life, and despite all the assistance my father gave her after we children reached maturity, I believe Mother would have been happier with her work if Dad had let her go out on her own limbs more often, instead of coaxing her back in. He did not want her working outside the home, for instance, or driving the car on family vacations, or traveling anywhere outside the city limits by herself.

So she silently stewed, I think, in our house on Eightieth Street and later in the little brick oven in Roebuck. She wanted to paint, but to paint would mean that she had abdicated her role as her father's "stupid" daughter. I don't believe it ever occurred to her, or perhaps occurred to her only late in life, that it was possible to be an artist and stupid at the same time—even necessary, perhaps.

Of course, the grain of stupidity Flannery O'Connor talks about as being essential to the mind of the artist (why look at anything too long if you already know exactly what it is and what it means?) was not the kind of stupidity my grandfather meant. I suspect he was the really stupid one—a vain, arrogant, violent man. He forced my mother to quit high school and work as a telephone operator while her sister went to college, but Mother became an obsessive reader, letter writer, and sympathetic listener to all but her children. In our case, there was simply too much she could not permit herself to hear.

I wish I had spoken to Mother on these points. But on that day so long ago, after the contentious lunch and my pronouncement that Jesus was a fag, Dad found Mom wandering the circle at Five Points South, still obsessing over Jesus' alleged pederasty with John.

Twenty-three years later, my friend Robert and I took down Dad's workshop. Dad was long dead, as were my brother Scotty and his son Michael; after ten years of being cared for by my brother Gary, Mom was in a nursing home, suffering from dementia; and Gary was more than happy to see the eyesore in the backyard dismantled.

"Dad is rolling over in his grave," Jeanie said at the time, because she knew Robert was gay.

But Jeanie also knew Dad would have appreciated the irony. He probably would have smiled, shaken his head, and said, "Now, if that don't beat all."

"My God," Robert said. "He didn't want this thing to ever come down, did he?"

I was holding the ladder while Robert pounded at overhead beams with a sledge hammer. "Nails," he gasped. "Your father must have spent a fortune on nails. And he used the kind that are barbed like fishhooks. Shit, I'm taking a break."

I went to get the lawn chairs and Gatorade. Robert had AIDS and was supposed to take it easy, avoid overexertion, stay out of the sun. But he ignored the rules from the first day on the job, though we did try to take regular breaks. We had a running joke about the relative merits of Gatorade and Powerade. It all depended on the color, we decided. Lemon-lime Powerade beat Gatorade hands down. But purple Powerade, the flavor called Arctic Blast, inevitably gave us the runs.

"Look at that thing," Robert said. He waved his cigarette in the direction of the workshop. "It's taken us three days, and all we've managed to do is knock down some plywood and get insulation up our butts. What did he think he was building this for, a nuclear war?"

"Dad didn't want a tornado to get it," I said. One had torn through the backyard in 1974, I added. It took down some trees and killed a man in Center Point.

"Well, I'm not surprised the tornado couldn't take it down," Robert said. "Not the way he built it. It's like he foresaw that some fag would try to take it apart one day."

Robert laughed through a cloud of smoke. "Let it never be said that I wasn't butch enough to do the job."

We finished off the Gatorade and girded ourselves again for the fight. At every point where two nails would have sufficed, Dad had hammered in four. If the job could have been done with nine-penny nails, Dad went with twelve. It did not help that the rafters, studs, beams, and joists had baked for nearly thirty years in the Alabama heat, rendering them hard as stone. Even with crowbars, sledge hammers, and a demonic commitment, Robert and I nearly killed ourselves taking apart my father's workshop.

The rewards, though, were immense. Each time I wrenched a nail from the wood, I imagined my father driving it in. He had taught me to use the weight of the hammer, to spare my wrist and elbows, to let my unconscious plot the hammer's flight, to trust my eyes instead of my brain, to stay focused but relaxed, and, most important, to enjoy the rhythm of honest work in the open air and light. He was a stickler for accurate measurements, for following directions, for using the best materials, except when they were overpriced. He taught me that the value of something built well outweighed its eventual use. In this sense, my father was a Platonist and therefore wouldn't have lasted long on the faculty of an American university at the close of the twentieth century. Thank God, that was the last thing he would have wanted in life.

Dad wanted a piece of the west. What he couldn't have at River Ranch, Florida, I was going to have on his behalf in Owyhee County, Idaho.

The night Robert and I finished taking down Dad's workshop, a section of framed two-by-fours fell on Robert's head. He dodged the most direct blow and sustained only scratches and a sore back. But I could hear the pain and desperation in his voice when he later called from destinations west. He and his friend Tom had volunteered to truck the pieces of workshop to its eventual resting place. Arkansas, Kansas, Colorado. It was their first trip west, an alternately romantic and disillusioning trek. Denver, which they'd anticipated with such fervor (it had the most gay bars west of the

Mississippi and east of San Francisco, they'd been told)
proved to be just another place to get anonymously
drunk. The bench seat of the truck was excruciating because of Robert's back; the lovely stretches of western
real estate couldn't compensate for the sly looks they'd
get in raw-boned small towns. There was, of course, the
sensation of spaciousness, of a frontier as yet without
limits, but this euphoria had to be counterbalanced by a
dead reckoning of pain and isolation. They bickered.
They medicated. They spent and drove and searched for
"docs-in-a-box" across the breadth of America. And
then they hit Idaho, Boise in particular, and, like Laura
and me, fell in love with the place.

"You're not going to believe this," Robert said, "but
Boise, Idaho, has the best gay bar I've ever been in."

This, despite the stories he'd heard. The gay-bashing.
The legal showdowns, the bloody tales from the '50s.
Robert and Tom fed the ducks and geese. They walked
along the river. And when I rendezvoused with them in
September to unload the truck, they were relaxed,
happy, and confident. They didn't seem to want to go
back to Alabama. Neither did I.

In fact, I was thinking about buying a horse. Bob
Vansickel had been keeping an eye out for one ever
since I told him that my daughters, especially Ashley,
liked horses. The plan was that Bob would find a suit-
ably gentle quarterhorse at auction, and I'd buy it from
him. It would be the Covington family horse. Bob

would care for it on his ranch and use it to herd cattle, but I'd hold the papers. And whenever we got up to Idaho, the horse would be waiting for us there.

Bob found the horse that fall. His name was Frankie, a strawberry roan with a sweet disposition and a tender mouth. I also bought a travel trailer. Land in Idaho, a travel trailer, a horse. Ashley taped a photograph of Frankie to the wall of her cubicle at the fine arts school in Birmingham she was attending that year. Frankie was her horse, she told her classmates, but I think she found it difficult to explain what he was doing two thousand miles away.

The first time I saw the horse, when Jim Neel and I went to Idaho to set and level the corners of the workshop's foundation, I didn't mount him but simply fed him hay. I didn't know a thing about horses. I tried to feed him an apple, a carrot. He looked at me as though I'd lost my mind.

Maybe I had.

In late October, I returned to Idaho to reinforce the foundation and put in the floor of the workshop-turned-cabin. It had been snowing, a blinding snow, so I finally had to stop working and settle into Thelma's ranch house for coffee and roasted Barbados goat.

Thelma was in a reflective mood. "Sometimes you run into people who are closer than your blood kin," she said. "There's something about looking at the same mountain and breathing the same air."

After lunch, the snow stopped, and Bob Vansickel suggested it was time to give Frankie a ride. One of his cowhands saddled the horse and gave me basic instructions. I settled and cinched my cowboy hat, hauled myself aboard, and took Frankie for some turns around the pasture.

"Go ahead," Bob said. "Take him on out. You're fine with him. He'll try to shake the bit out, but don't worry about that."

So I rode Frankie out to Bates Creek Road and down it toward my land. I tested him with the heels of my cowboy boots. He broke into a gallop. It was fine. And when I knew he was responding to my commands, I turned him off the road and headed up the hill toward Coyote Point. By this time, it had started to snow again. I didn't know whether it was the right thing to do, to take Frankie off the road and into the sagebrush and rocks, the steep incline. But I was possessed, and he seemed to know it. He found his own way to the top, to the very spot where I was erecting my father's workshop. The entire valley spread before us and the Owyhee Mountains loomed beyond, freshly white. The snowflakes were light and feathery. A plume of exhaled air rose from Frankie's nostrils like smoke. I leaned forward and patted his neck. And just like in the movies, he pawed the desert sand, took a sideways step, shook his head, and neighed.

Are you at the good part yet?

Back at the Ranch

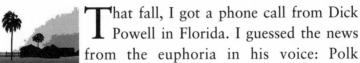That fall, I got a phone call from Dick Powell in Florida. I guessed the news from the euphoria in his voice: Polk County Circuit Court Judge Robert A. Young had finally declared Powell's easements good, and the decision had been upheld on appeal by a three-judge panel. It had been thirty-nine years since the easements were recorded at the Polk County Courthouse, twenty years since Powell began his campaign on behalf of the landowners at River Ranch. Since most of these original landowners, including my father, had died, it was a victory for their memory and for the generation that would now pass the land on to the generation that would follow them.

Apparently, the Hunt Club hadn't taken the news well. "You should have seen those idiots," Powell said. "They went ape-shit, hollering and carrying on."

The club had one strategy left. Through their attorneys, Pete and Sandy Edwards had asked Judge Young to conduct an evidentiary hearing to determine whether there were grounds to reconsider his original decision. If the decision held up under this ancillary challenge, the cow man's fence would have to come down, and Powell could use the driveway he'd bulldozed to his property no matter what the Hunt Club or the sheriff's department or anybody else had to say.

It was a different Pete Edwards who slouched into the hearing room on that bright December day. The president of the Hunt Club was wearing a blue-plaid western-style shirt and jeans, but he was missing his belt with the enormous silver buckle, and he did not have on his cowboy boots or Stetson. He seemed pale and subdued, a much older man than the one I had seen addressing the Hunt Club at the old Frostproof High School auditorium or greeting his fellow hunters at the start of hog season after my canvas house had been shot up.

We shook hands, but I wasn't sure Pete remembered me exactly, even though he said, "I know who you are."

Dick Powell, on the other hand, had been expecting me. He'd called to give me the date, place, and time. We didn't make a public show of our alliance, though. A smile and nod across the table were sufficient. But when Sandy Edwards saw that Powell and I knew each other, she gave me a sour look.

Among the witnesses called before Judge Young were a representative from Avatar, the holding company that had survived GAC's bankruptcy and still owned considerable acreage at River Ranch, and Tommie Ferrell, a real estate development specialist employed by the Division of Florida Land Sales.

The Avatar representative denied Pete Edwards' claim that Gulf American, or its successors, GAC and Avatar, had ever turned over control of River Ranch to the Hunt Club.

Tommie Ferrell, who had prepared the Division of Florida Land Sales' *River Ranch Acres Investigative Report*, testified there had been numerous complaints from landowners that the Hunt Club had denied them access to their land. In fact, Ferrell had personally witnessed an elderly couple being denied access. Members of the Hunt Club had even hassled Ferrell at the main gate.

Despite the investigators' conclusion that River Ranch landowners did, indeed, have "legal access" to their property, it was Ferrell's opinion that the Division of Florida Land Sales could not enforce "physical access." The division's jurisdiction, she said, extended only to the question of the registration of easements. The easements appeared to be good. The rest was up to the courts. The division's report had not recommended any further action.

It was, she explained, "a dangerous situation. . . . We didn't want anyone to get hurt."

When Pete Edwards was called, he denied that the Hunt Club had ever prevented landowners from entering River Ranch. The gate had been put in there, he said, "to protect the land." He acknowledged that the Hunt Club had collected about $90,000 during the previous year in fees from members and guests using the gate. It had also taken in about $20,000 in cattle leases.

But then he put his hand to his head. "I'm getting a little dizzy," he said. He added that he was on medication, at which point his attorney motioned for him to be quiet.

Embedded in Pete's testimony, though, was a hint of defeat. "If it's their property, they can camp on it," he said at one point.

And so, after all these years, the bitter legal struggle appeared to be ending with a relative whimper. Once again, Judge Young upheld the validity of Powell's easement. The cow man's fence and the Hunt Club's gates would have to come down.

In a July 1999 letter, Powell's attorney summed it up nicely: "Sometimes the good guys win!"

But there were still those camps with names like "Camp Run-a-Muck," "Hawg Heaven," and "Leisure Village at Armadillo Bay." Thousands of Hunt Club members and guests continued to descend on River Ranch each year, and hundreds of their structures, which had been illegally erected on other people's property, still stood. What would happen to them?

The state of Florida appeared to have an answer.

For years, Florida had been the nation's leader in acquiring and preserving ecologically sensitive tracts of land through condemnation or outright purchase under the state's CARL (Conservation and Recreational Lands) program. And state biologists had consistently ranked River Ranch Acres at the top of their list of desirable properties. The acreage was unrivaled in terms of ecological diversity and susceptibility to development. River Ranch was home to the largest nesting population of bald eagles in the lower forty-eight states and provided habitat for other endangered species like the red-cockaded woodpecker, the Florida panther, and the gopher tortoise. It also contained some of the rarest species of plants and insects on the North American continent.

But each year, when the CARL committee, composed of representatives from six state agencies, met to vote on which properties to purchase, River Ranch came up short.

"We were scared to go down there," one committee member told me. "We were afraid we'd get shot."

The last time the proposal had come up for consideration, only two of the six members had voted to purchase River Ranch. "Fish and Game wouldn't touch it," said state zoologist Katy NeSmith. "It was too messy."

This year, the committee was more evenly divided. When Dick Powell appeared before them, the representative from Community Affairs asked him why state ownership would make Pete Edwards and the Hunt Club go away. "He sounds like somebody who's willing to go against the state," the representative said.

Another committee member described Edwards as a "jack-booted thug," and said, "Let's not get our foot stuck in this mess."

But Powell, Katy NeSmith, and Gary Knight, NeSmith's boss at the Florida Natural Areas Inventory, wouldn't give up.

"It's a great opportunity for the state to correct a wrong," Knight said. "For all those property owners to be intimidated is just outrageous."

Committee member Ruark Cleary, of the Florida Environmental Protection Agency, agreed. "It would be a terrible crime not to try to preserve this enormous piece of land in central Florida," he said. "It would be a disservice not to give it a shot."

If approved, the state purchase of River Ranch would result in a wildlife corridor of 217,000 contiguous acres down the center of Florida. It would be the largest wilderness area within a two-hour drive of Tampa, for instance, and would be consonant with federal efforts to restore the natural drainage of the Kissimmee River and protect the groundwater of the vast Floridian aquifer.

The lobbying and testimony of Powell, NeSmith, and Knight finally bore fruit when the committee voted unanimously to recommend River Ranch for purchase. The news sent shock waves through an already battered Hunt Club hierarchy.

"They can't keep us out of there," Pete Edwards is reported to have said. "We're going to fight the state. I own property in there. I bought it to take a gun in there, and that's what I'm going to do."

Alan Ingram, who had briefly replaced Pete as president of the Hunt Club, was incensed to learn that Dick Powell had testified before the committee. "He's a professional con artist. We've been fighting him for years."

And as for this so-called camouflage man, who was rumored to be roaming the back roads of River Ranch at night, Ingram had a warning: "People are saying if they see him and he doesn't stop, they're gonna shoot him."

Still, even after the courts upheld the validity of Dick Powell's easements, and even after the CARL committee recommended that the state of Florida protect the land through outright purchase, the Hunt Club wasn't completely out of the picture.

"There's talk of giving the Hunt Club a piece of the property," said Gary Knight.

Insiders within the state political machinery had seen the opportunity for a deal. Shortly after they got wind of the state's interest in purchasing land at River Ranch, a wealthy attorney, Irving Wheeler, let it be known that he would buy any River Ranch property for $400 an acre. The attorney's agent in this matter, Dean Saunders, a former state senator and friend of the Hunt Club, had assured Wheeler that the state would be willing to pay no less than $600 an acre, which was the property's tax-assessed value. By consolidating parcels at the lower price, Wheeler could make a quick profit of over $2 million, assuming the sale to the state went smoothly. To grease the wheels, Dean Saunders offered to broker an arrangement by which Hunt Club members who were squatting on other people's land would be able to keep their camps intact. The state might own the rest of River Ranch, but the squatters' camps would remain on the land in perpetuity. In Newsletter 52 of the River Ranch Landowners Association, Dick Powell wrote that when he met with a representative of the Nature Conservancy, which had been selected by the state to negotiate the purchase of River Ranch property, the representative said, "The state of Florida is not interested in buying any land with access problems, or with cows or hunting shacks on it."

Powell said he "assured the representative that the problem with the cows and access had been taken care of through the judicial system; however, the problem of the shacks was yet to be resolved."

The solution to that problem came as a surprise to everyone.

Nobody knows how the fire started. What's recorded is that it was a small fire by central Florida standards, only 368 acres. The Florida State Division of Forestry responded with two tank engines and a helicopter. It was nothing on the scale of the 3,000-acre fire that had swept through River Ranch two summers before. But the May 2000 River Ranch fire, because of the dense palmetto, proved difficult to contain. The drought had been intense all across Florida, with conditions compounded by low humidity and high temperatures. Larger fires were burning the same day ten miles west of Port Charlotte, in the remote swampland of Osceola County, and in the Apalachicola National Forest, forty miles southwest of Tallahassee. But the River Ranch fire was the most contentious and destructive.

Whether ignited by lightning or carelessness or arson (some suspected the mythic camouflage man), the fire spread quickly through the heart of the Hunt Club's self-proclaimed camping area. Resin-filled pine trees exploded when the heat reached them, showering the trailers and cabins with flaming branches, needles, and cones. Paint peeled from the sides of rooftop water barrels. Burning swamp buggy tires threw a thick corona of smoke around the sun. By the time firefighters finally brought the blaze under control, at least 113 of the Hunt Club's structures had been destroyed, more than a quarter of a million dollars in official damage exacted, and much more to be tallied later if the squatters who owned the shacks could be found.

But the land my father had given me was untouched—a vast field of palmetto and pine, as fine as beaten silver under the first light of dawn. My shot-up canvas house and accordioned Jeep stood as they had always stood, memorials to the crazy idea that any inheritance might be worth claiming, no matter how small, no matter the cost.

Down the road from my place, however, the devastation was complete, and the camps belonging to the Mirees and many of their fellow hog hunters had been reduced to smoldering ash.

The good part? Maybe. But what about our lives?

Epilogue

Bob Vansickel and Thelma Rumsey have sold Kamaloops Ranch out in Idaho. Thelma has moved back to her family's place at Silver Lake. She took with her Frankie, the Covington horse, which I traded to her for an old house trailer that still sits, as far as I know, in the valley beneath Coyote Point. Rumor has it that Bob Vansickle has found a new business partner, another widow on another ranch in another county northwest of Oreana. Some say he has found the Lord.

The wind blew down my father's workshop on Coyote Point. I guess it's just as well. My desire to make a killing in real estate ended in bankruptcy, and the land, both there and in Florida, was put into the hands of a trustee assigned by the court. I have just learned, though, that the bankruptcy proceedings are over, my debts have been discharged, and the trustee decided not to sell the land after all. He said it wasn't worth enough for him to fool with. "Nuisance money" was the expression he used.

It's not exactly the way I would have liked this story to end, but it seems to me that the good part of a story doesn't have much to do with the way it ends. The good part comes earlier than that. Sometimes the good part is not even in the story. Sometimes the good part is what has been left out.

For me, it was the day I got the GPS personal navigator. I had bought it in order to locate the Florida land Dad had deeded to me, but first I had to initialize the device in Birmingham by sending a signal to distant satellites. I'd read the manual carefully, and I was impressed by the simple logic that underlay the technology. To find out how to get where you're going, you have to know where you are. To find out where you are, you have to know where you've been.

As my first reference point, I chose the fifty-yard line of the practice field at the university where I taught, because this was the closest place I could think of with an unobstructed view of the sky. I held the device aloft and turned it on. Then I waited for it to find the satellites and for the satellites to send back my position, correct to within thirty feet of where I stood. When the coordinates arrived, I instructed the device to save them, and I keyed in a name for this spot in the middle of a football field. I called it "Work."

Getting into my River Ranch–bound Jeep, I positioned the GPS device on the dashboard. I cranked the engine and headed to one of my old neighborhoods. There I saved the coordinates and typed in "Five Points South."

Next, I drove to the top of Red Mountain, where Vulcan stood, the god of the fire and the forge. I pulled to the side of the road long enough to save the coordinates and type in the statue's name.

Then I descended into Homewood, the neighborhood where Vicki and I and our daughters lived. It had been a cool, dry spring. The ornamental cherry trees were in full bloom. I pulled up in front of a yellow, two-story house on a familiar cul-de-sac. Bikes lay on their side in the yard. Through the front windows of the house, I could see Ashley at the computer. She was either working on a story set in El Salvador or tracing our genealogy on the Internet. In the living room, Laura and a friend of hers were rehearsing a dance number for their upcoming production of *Grease*. They must have turned the bass all the way up. I thought I could feel the vibration inside the Jeep.

Suddenly the front door opened, and Vicki let out the cats, two gray, one white. I knew it was her by her shining hair. I waved, but I don't think she saw me before she closed the door again. I got out of the Jeep and stood in the front yard with my GPS device in hand. I held it chest-high and level. I told myself I was on a mission to claim my father's dream. Somewhere high above my head, satellites were hurtling through space, beaming my position to me. I saved the coordinates and named the place "Home." Then I walked inside.

Acknowledgments

The author would like to thank Rosalie Siegel for her faithfulness; Sarah McNally, Dawn Seferian, and Don Fehr for their inexhaustible patience; Jeanie Wolaver, Gary Covington, and Vicki, Ashley, and Laura Covington for their unfailing love.

This book could not have been written without the help of these good friends in Alabama: Jim and Lynn Neel, Bill Murray, Joey and Veronica Kennedy, Charles Wolaver, Craig Wolaver, Steve Sexton, Marilyn Kurata, Juanita Sizemore, Bonnie Armour, Jeffrey Cohn, Jake Reiss, Robert Watts, Wayne Cook, Bill Whetstone, Brodie and Adair Whetstone, Grace Reid, Nathan Weiss, Mysti Garner, Bob Clayton, and Jane Mitchell.

And these in Florida: Jim and Claire Marsh, Dick Powell, W. A. Read, Katy NeSmith, and Dale Chambliss.

And these in Oregon, Idaho, Georgia, Iowa, and New York: Thelma Rumsey, Bob Vansickle, Walt and Barbara Watkins, John and Jean Gabica, Mitch and Cyndi Wieland, Norbert and Ben Wieland, Judy Lees, Mary Swander, Howard Cruse, and Ed Sedarbaum.

Many thanks to all of you.